AF496757

THE

CHARTER AND STATUTES

OF

JEFFERSON COLLEGE,

WASHINGTON, MISSISSIPPI,

AS

REVISED AND AMENDED:

TOGETHER WITH

A HISTORICAL SKETCH OF THE INSTITUTION

FROM ITS ESTABLISHMENT TO THE PRESENT TIME:

———

TO WHICH IS PREFIXED

A LIST OF THE TRUSTEES, OFFICERS AND FACULTY,
THE ACTS OF CONGRESS AND OF THE LEGIS-
LATURE RELATING TO THE INSTITUTION,

AND A

CATALOGUE OF ITS LIBRARY,

APPARATUS, &c.

———

PUBLISHED BY ORDER OF THE BOARD OF TRUSTEES.

———

NATCHEZ:
PRINTED AT THE BOOK AND JOB OFFICE,
MAIN STREET, NEAR THE POST OFFICE.
....
1840.

TRUSTEES OF JEFFERSON COLLEGE.
MAY 1, 1839.

THE GOVERNOR OF THE STATE,
Ex officio President of the Board.

1. JOHN T. GRIFFITH, Vice President.
2. LEVIN WAILES, Secretary.
3. B. L. C. WAILES, Treasurer.

4. A. L. BINGAMAN,
5. J. W. BRYAN,
6. F. L. CLAIBORNE,
7. WM. C. CONNER,
8. LEVIN COVINGTON,
9. G. L. C. DAVIS,
10. STEPHEN DUNCAN,
11. THOMAS FARRAR,
12. THOMAS FREELAND,
13. PHILIP HOGGATT,
14. NATHANIEL HOGGATT,
15. ANDREW MACRERY,
16. JOHN T. McMURRAN,
17. JAMES McCALEB,
18. ALEX. MONTGOMERY,
19. J. W. MONETTE,
20. GEORGE NEWMAN,
21. JOHN A. QUITMAN,
22. HORATIO N. SMITH,
23. WILLIAM STANTON,
24. WHITE TURPIN,
25. RICHARD S. WILLIAMS,

FACULTY OF JEFFERSON COLLEGE.

REV. A. STEPHENS, President, Professor of Moral and Intellectual Philosophy, Belles Lettres, &c.—Salary, $3,000.

REV. A. STEPHENS, Professor of Ancient Languages.

LEONARD D. GALE, M. D., Professor of Natural and Experimental Philosophy, Chemistry, and Mineralogy.—Salary $2,000.

JACOB AMMEN, Professor of Mathematics, Civil Engineering, and Superintendent of the Military Department.—Salary, $2,000.

————————————, Professor of Drawing, Painting, and Lithography.—Salary, 2,000.

J. A. T. MIDDERHOFF, Professor of Modern Languages, and Assistant Professor of Ancient Languages.—Salary, $2,000.

PREPARATORY DEPARTMENT.

————————————, Principal of the Preparatory Department.—Salary $1,000.

REV. WM. WHIELDEN, Assistant Instructor in the Preparatory Department, and Librarian.—Salary, $900.

TERMS OF TUITION.

For Students in the College proper, per session of five months, $25 00
"   "   "   Preparatory Department, per session,   15 00
There will be no extra charges, except the matriculation and graduating fees.

BOARD, &c.

For Boarding, per month,   -   -   -   -   - $15 00
For Washing, per month,   -   -   .   .   .   -   2 00
Use of bed and bedding, when furnished by the Steward, per
    month,   2 00
For candles, per month, during the first session,   50
For   do.   "   during the second, or winter session,   75
For fuel during the first session one dollar, and for the second session
    four dollars, making five dollars per annum.
    Tuition and board will be required in advance for each session.

ADDRESS TO THE PUBLIC.

The Trustees of Jefferson College, at Washington, Mississippi, have the satisfaction to announce to the public, that the Institution is now prepared for the reception of students. Upon its reorganization, some exposition of its prospects will be naturally expected, and it is with great satisfaction that the Trustees are enabled to declare, that at no period of its history have their anticipations been so sanguine as to its stability and success.

On the past it is in vain to look back, except so far as retrospection may enable us to perceive and avoid former errors. The causes which have combined to retard its active usefulness, whether to be traced to inexperience in its organization, to difference of opinion as to government and discipline, or to the want of funds, and the consequent difficulty of retaining a sufficient number of competent professors, no longer exist. The funds of the institution are now available, being either in bank stock, bank credits, or promissory notes secured by mortgage. Commodious buildings are prepared for the Faculty and Students. The most able professors within the knowledge of the Trustees, have been engaged for every branch of education; and a primary school is established upon a liberal foundation. The Steward's department, it is believed, in all essential details, is addressed to present exigencies, and is in charge of an individual in all respects competent to its duties. In fine, nothing within the experience or resources of the Trustees, has been deferred, which is demanded by the moral, intellectual, or physical necessities of the student. A brief, but more specific detail of the course of discipline and study, and some notice of the distinguished individuals whom it has been the good fortune of the Trustees to engage, may be desirable to the people, and advantageous to the institution.

I. At the head of the College is the Reverend A. Stephens, who fills the chair of Ancient Languages. In this gentleman are united the accomplishments of a thorough Philologist and an elegant Belles Lettres scholar. He filled the chair of Ancient Languages in the University of Nashville with brilliant reputation. In addition to the high commendations of President Lindsley of that institution (sufficient, in themselves to place the abilities of their subject beyond all cavil) he is among the first to carry into successful practice in our Colleges, if not to introduce, the recent improvements by German Scholars in Philology, which has reduced in an extraordinary manner, the irregularities of the Greek grammar; and his Address upon the effects of education, and their influence on our republican institutions, have elicited the general admiration of the first scholars and critics of the nation.

, The classical course under his direction will be conducted upon the most recent and improved plans, precisely similar to those established in the best American, English and German Universities. He will have the aid of an Assistant Professor of Ancient Languages of established reputation as a very successful instructor.

To the President is also committed the departments of Rhetoric and Belles Lettres, of Intellectual and Moral Philosophy, and their kindred branches.

In the former, to the study of the standard and established authors, will be added the improvements of Whately, including Logic; and in Philosophy, the tenets of Locke and his school, designated as the sensual system, will not be entirely followed, but the corrections of later writers of Scotland, Germany, and France will be adopted. The Student will be aided in his researches by the views of Seward, Reid, Kant and Cousin, and the eclectic system of the last named Philosopher will be the basis of the course.

Under the supervision of the President, also, the classes are to be thoroughly exercised in composition, declamation and debate; branches of study which under our free institutions are indispensable to every citizen, and which have at all times been but too much neglected.

II. In Mathematics and Mathematical Physics, the system of the Military Academy at West Point, and the Polytechnic School at Paris, will be adopted as far as practicable.

Professor Ammen, the gentleman to whom this department is committed, is a graduate of West Point; and was afterwards engaged for several years as instructor there, and in this capacity was distinguished for his efficiency and thoroughness. He brings with him a system of study and government, which has exalted that cherished school of the nation, to a rank with the most distinguished institutions in Europe. He will also have charge of the department of Engineering, for which he is eminently fitted, not only by an excellent elementary education, but by practical experience on the most important public works. Surveying is another essential branch of study, which will be superintended by the same individual, and will be not only taught through the medium of books, but practically illustrated by instruments in the field.

III. The department of Chemistry and Experimental Philosophy, is under the charge of Professor Leonard D. Gale, M. D. a gentleman in whom are united, various and rare qualifications for the Professorship to which he has been appointed. The language of a friend, but of a competent judge, thus speaks of those qualifications: " Devoted from early life to the pursuits to which he has given himself, brought up in the laboratories of those distinguished men, Silliman and Torry, bred to the profession of medicine, addicted to the most industrious and laborious study of the secrets of nature, of great experience as an instructor and manipulator, the discoverer of several new chemical substances, an accomplished mineralogist, an able practical geologist, and a good botanist, he will be an ornament and an acquisition to the Institution and the State." Chemistry will be taught upon the most approved plans, and illustrated by practical experiments, with which the students will be themselves familiarized. Instruction in mineralogy and geology, branches of education every day gaining importance and favor, will be given with the aid of a cabinet of minerals and fossils, with which the Professor is amply provided. Exploring excursions will be made by him in company with the students for practical experiments: and botany and natural history, so nearly allied, will, on such occasions as opportunity permits, become objects of study and explanation.

IV. Instruction in the modern languages will be given by Professor Midderhoff, a native of Prussia, and a graduate of a German University. It is only necessary to state, that this gentleman is very favorably known in this community, where he has been successfully engaged in teaching for the last two years, and is remarkable for the tact with which he imparts knowledge. The French, German and Spanish languages will be taught by him after the most approved method.

V. The accomplishment of drawing will be taught by a Professor fully competent to the duties of his station. Delineation of the elements of the human figure, landscape, sketches from nature, topography and lithography upon the most approved principles, will be included in his course.

VI. In addition to the stated studies above detailed, will be added, lectures upon internal and constitutional law, political economy, finance and modern history as a part of the regular course.

VII. The branches of study thus enumerated, will all be required of undergraduates, except engineering, drawing, and the modern languages, which will be optional, with the sanction of parents or guardians and the Faculty. Students not desirous of obtaining degrees, will be privileged, under the advice of the Faculty, to select the studies they may wish to pursue, and will be entitled to testimonials of the attainments they have made in such branches.

VIII. For exercise, in place of gymnastics, the military drill will be substituted, and practised daily by all students. For the attainment or preservation of health, and the acquisition of graceful motion and manly bearing, no means have been found superior in its results, or more agreeable to the student.

IX. A military police for the preservation of good order and regularity, will be established and enforced, so far as the paramount objects
of the institution will permit.

With the advantages thus offered to the student in every department
of science, and with the exceptions of a rigid College course, in favor
of those whose age, circumstances or disposition disincline them to
toil for the entire honors of the institution, it is confidently believed
that the views of the whole community will be amply met. The provision made for the instruction of one student from each county in the
State, whose circumstances will not admit of their paying for the College course, is upon the most liberal scale, and has heretofore been sub-
mitted to the public. The location of the College Hall is healthful.
The moral and religious influences which will be brought to bear
upon the inmates, cannot but be salutary, and it is not hazaiding too
much to say that the opportunities for acquiring a solid and useful education, are not surpassed in any institution west of the mountains. The
patronage and support of Mississippians is especially desirable, not more
for the honor of the State, than for the advantages that must accrue to
the rising generation.

To the young of whatever nation, *home education and home discipline,* are of lasting moment, Destined, as they are, at no distant day
to direct the government of the country, it is essential that they should
be identified with their fellow-citizens; that they should imbibe public
opinion, and be imbued with the spirit of the laws which wisdom and
experience have framed for the prosperity of the State.

At this very moment, a formidable contest has commenced between
the North and the South, from the possible results of which the eye
of the patriot instinctively revolts. The issue can only be known to
the great Disposer of all things: but it surely becomes us to preserve
our children from any influence that might mislead their judgment or
weaken their patriotism. To do this effectually, WE MUST KEEP THEM
AT HOME!

A useful writer has said, that "the mother is the proper and only
source from which an infant should derive its nourishment." How
aptly does this beautiful sentiment apply to States and Nations! Let
no sordid nurse supply that food which a mother can give. The health
of your offspring may be endangered, and physical and moral evils
engendered, against which the carefulness, the vigilance, and tender-
ness of a mother are ever active to guard. So when the mind of this
infant is developing, and it asks for *intellectual sustenance,* let not its
country, its second mother, through negligence of the means of home
instruction, or unfounded prejudice, banish it to distant shores, to the
guidance of aliens and strangers. Their institutions may be blessed
with all that wealth, and science, and reputation can bestow; but *it is
the moral influence, after all, that makes the man;* the presence of

parents, kindred, and friends, and the serene and salutary influences which these relations exercise on every human heart.

Send your sons to other States, where they are released from social bonds, you not only cut off these powerful incentives to emulation, but you do more and worse; you weaken or detach the growing virtues of the heart, which have their spring and their support in affection lavished and reciprocated. You estrange them from their native land, youthful associations are forgotten, standards of morals and manners uncongenial with our feelings and our institutions are engendered; and patriotism, that much abused word, the *Amor Patriæ* of ancient Rome, has no portion in the soul.

To complete the delineation, is it not to be apprehended, that such a victim of mistaken views of education, with a head perverted by superficial acquirements, but with a heart presenting only a moral waste, may return to his parents corrupted by evil example, consumed by fierce passions, or degraded by brutalizing habits?

Persuaded that the moral influence of family associations, is of inestimable value, and that every other advantage is dearly purchased by its sacrifice, the Trustees have deeply at heart the prosperity of the Institution. They anxiously desire that auspicious day, when Mississippi will not be constrained to part from her children, but that parental solicitude may exert its vigilance at that most interesting period of their lives, when the mind begins to develope and the generous impulses of their hearts call for sympathy and. communion, and at a moment particularly, when these youthful emotions claim protection against the strong assault of the passions, which alas! for the imperfections of humanity, need no discipline to develope their fearful energies; but spring at once full-armed giants from the same soil where infant virtues sustain so feeble an existence.

With this rapid sketch of the condition and prospects of the College, and this exposition of the views of the Trustees, they confidently offer to the States of the South-West a participation in its benefits.

And now having performed their duty to the best of their ability, they commit the Institution to the learning, judgment, and fidelity of the Faculty, and have only, in conclusion, to invoke the blessing of a beneficent Providence upon this renewed effort in the cause of science and virtue.

ACTS OF THE LEGISLATURES

OF THE

TERRITORY AND STATE OF MISSISSIPPI,

IN RELATION TO

JEFFERSON COLLEGE.

AN ACT

To establish a College in the Mississippi Territory, Passed May 13th, 1802. Revised Code, page 410.

Whereas, Education conduces to the happiness and improvement of man, and is particularly necessary to the support and purity of Republican Governments; therefore,

SECTION 1. *Be it enacted by the Legislative Council and House of Representatives of the Mississippi Territory, in General Assembly convened,* That there shall be established in this Territory a College which shall bear the name of *Jefferson College,* in honor of Thomas Jefferson, President of the United States, and President of the American Philosophical Society.

SEC. 2. The following persons, to wit: William C. C. Claiborne, Anthony Hutchins, William Dunbar, of Second Creek, Benjamin Farrar, William Vousden, John Ellis, David Kerr, Adam Bingaman, David Lattimore, Bernard Lintot, Cato West, John Girault, Thomas M. Green, Samuel Gibson, Daniel Burnett, Felix Hughes, Alexander Montgomery, Drury W. Brazeale, Thomas Calvitt, James Caller, Nathaniel Christmass, John Steel, Abner Green, Sutton Banks, Abram Ellis, Richard Butler, Robert Dunbar, John McGrew, Jacob Stampley, Joseph Pannell, Isaac Guillard, John Bisland, Abraham Green, and James Hoggatt, shall be a body corporate by the name of "The Trustees of Jefferson College," and by that name shall be capable in law, to receive all donations, and recover all debts, which shall become the property of said College: and may in general do all acts for the benefit of the institution which are incident to bodies corporate.

Sec. 3. The first meeting of the Trustees, shall be held on the first Monday in January next, at the town of Washington, where they shall proceed to choose out of their own body, a President and Vice President. The President, or in his absence the Vice President, shall have power to call extraordinary meetings of the Trustees, by giving ten days notice to each member before such meeting shall be held. The ordinary meetings of the Board shall be held on their own adjournments. Thirteen members shall constitute a quorum to do business at the first meeting; but at all subsequent meetings, seven may constitute a quorum to proceed to business. The President, or in his absence from the meeting, the Vice President shall preside, or in case of the absence of both, any member chosen by a majority of the members present, shall preside.

Whereas, it is necessary, that on extraordinary occasions, the Board of Trustees of Jefferson College, should be called together at a short notice, and whereas, the mode provided for that purpose would often be attended with great delay; therefore,

Be it enacted, That the President of the Board of Trustees of Jefferson College, or in his absence from the Territory, the Vice President shall have authority to call a meeting of the Trustees at any time, provided notice shall be given of such intended meeting, by advertising the same in one of the newspapers of this Territory, twelve days before the said meeting shall be held.

Sec. 4. The Board of Trustees shall have power, and it shall be their duty, with all convenient speed, to fix on some healthy and central situation, whereat to establish the College, and to contract for the erecting of the necessary buildings. They shall also have power to engage a President and other Professors,—a Treasurer, and all necessary officers for conducting the civil and literary concerns of the College, and to displace and supersede them at pleasure. They also shall have authority, and it shall be their duty, to examine the proficiency of the students, and to confer the degrees of Bachelor and Master of Arts; to make all laws and regulations which they shall judge necessary for the good government of the College, and for promoting morality and virtue among the students. They shall take effectual care that students of all denominations may, and shall be admitted to equal advantages of a liberal education, and to the emoluments and honors of the College, and that they shall receive a like fair and generous treatment, during their residence thereat.

Sec. 5. In case of death, removal from the Territory, resignation, or refusal to act of any of the said Trustees, the Board may at any of their meetings appoint a successor.

Sec. 6. As Jefferson College must for the present be supported by the voluntary contributions of citizens, the Board of Trustees are authorized to raise for the benefit of said College, by lottery, a sum not exceeding ten thousand dollars. They shall also collect donations, from the citizens of the Territory and elsewhere. The names of such donors with their donations annexed, shall be inscribed in a book kept for that purpose, and shall be preserved among the archives of the College, in order that posterity may know who were the benefactors of the institution.

SEC. 7. The President, Professors, Tutors, and Students of the College, shall be exempt from all militia duty, during their continuance as members of the College; except in a general invasion of the Territory.

SEC. 8. The lands, public buildings, and other property belonging to Jefferson College, are hereby declared to be free from every kind of public tax.

AN ACT

To establish a permanent Site for Jefferson College. Passed 11th November, 1803.

Whereas, The Board of Trustees of Jefferson College, by their petition, dated the 25th of July last, prayed the Legislature to establish by law, the site of Jefferson College in such position as is set forth in said petition:

SECTION 1. *Be it therefore enacted by the Legislative Council and House of Representatives of the Mississippi Territory, in General Assembly convened,* That a certain donation or parcel of land, including a spring commonly called Ellicott's spring, presented by John and James Foster, and Randal Gibson, to the said Board of Trustees of Jefferson College, for the use of the said College, and such other adjoining parcel of land to be procured by the said Board, situated in the vicinage of the town of Washington, shall together constitute a lot, within the limits of which shall be erected the buildings of the said College, and which said lot is hereby declared to be the permanent site of Jefferson College. Revised Code, page 412.

By the 2d Section of an Act of the Legislature of the Mississippi Territory, passed the 13th of December, 1811, in relation to escheats, it is enacted that "All property that may escheat under this act during the term of ten years, shall be vested in the Trustees of Jefferson College, for the use and benefit of said College."—(See Turner's Digest, page 264.)

The privilege granted by the above act, expired on the 13th of December, 1821.

AN ACT

To amend an Act to incorporate the Trustees of Jefferson College.
Passed 23d December, 1812.

SECTION 1. *Be it enacted by the Legislative Council and House
of Representatives of the Mississippi Territory, in General Assembly
convened,* That a quorum of the Board of Trustees of Jefferson College, named in the second section of the Act, to which this is an
amendment, and such other members of the said Board, as have been
duly elected, or hereafter may be elected, conformably to the first section of the said act, to which this is an amendment, and their successors, be, and they are hereby, declared to be a body corporate and poli-
tic, capable in law to do and perform all things incident to the bodies
corporate, both in law and equity.

SEC. 2. The Board of Trustees of Jefferson College, shall at no
time exceed forty in number, and the said Board shall, at their discre-
tion, proceed to elect members to make up that number.

SEC. 3. The Trustees of said College, shall have power to establish stated meetings of the said Board. Revised Code, page 412.

AN ACT

To amend an Act entitled "An Act to establish a College in the Mississippi Territory." Passed 13th December, 1816.

SECTION 1. *Be it enacted by the Legislative Council and House
of Representatives of the Mississippi Territory, in General Assembly
convened,* That for the purpose of aiding Jefferson College in carrying
on the operations of the institution, the sum of six thousand dollars shall
be, and the same is hereby loaned to the said College for the term of
five years, to be paid to the President of the said College, in four equal
annual instalments, to wit: one thousand, five hundred dollars on the
first day of January, 1817, 1818, 1819, and 1820, which money shall
be used by the said College, in the employment of one or more Teachers, or Professors for the institution, and it shall be the duty of the
Territorial Treasurer, to take from the Trustees of the College, under
the seal of the College, used in their corporate name, bond in double
the amount of each of said instalments, payable to the Governor of
the Mississippi Territory, and his successors in office, conditioned for
the payment of the said instalments, respectively, in five years from the
date of the said bond, and also a mortgage to secure the payment thereof, on such real estate of said College, as the said Treasurer may require; and it shall also be the duty of the said Treasurer, to cause said
bonds and mortgages to be proven, and recorded in the office of the
Register of the Orphan's Court, of the county of Adams, immediately

after the execution of such bonds and mortgages, respectively, and thereafter to keep the same among the papers of the Treasury; which bonds and mortgages shall be put in suit by the said Treasurer, on the breach of the condition thereof, in any court of competent jurisdiction.

(Here follows a clause making a donation to Greene Academy, and St. Stephen's Academy, each of the sum of $500.)

SEC. 2. If any Trustee shall fail to attend the said Board, for four stated meetings in succession, it shall be deemed and considered a refusal to act as such within the meaning of this act, and the Board shall proceed to appoint a successor to such Trustee: *Provided*, that the provisions of this section shall not extend to any Trustee, who at the time of such failure be sick and unable to attend, or temporarily absent from the territory.

SEC. 3. It shall be the duty of the President of the Board of Trustees, for the time being, to report annually to the General Assembly at the commencement of the session, the state and condition of the College, and the amount of active funds in the possession of the corporation at the time of making such report. Revised code, page 413.

AN ACT

To authorize a loan of money to the Trustees of Jefferson College. Passed 12th February, 1820.

SECTION 1. *Be it enacted by the Senate and House of Representatives of the State of Mississippi, in General Assembly convened,* That the sum of four thousand dollars, at an interest at the rate of six per centum per annum, shall be, and the same is hereby loaned to the Trustees of Jefferson College, for the term of five years, which money shall be used by the said Trustees, in completing the left wing of the said College, and the said sum shall be paid to the President of the said Board by the Treasurer of the State, upon his executing a bond under the seal of the College, used in their corporate name, in the sum of eight thousand dollars, payable to the Governor of the State, and his successors in office, conditioned for the payment of the said sum of four thousand dollars, with interest as aforesaid, in five years from the date of the said bond, and also a mortgage to secure the payment thereof, on such real estate of the said College, as the said Treasurer may require; and it shall be the duty of the said Treasurer, to cause said bond and mortgage to be proven, and recorded in the office of the clerk of the County Court, for the county of Adams, immediately after the execution thereof, and thereafter to keep the same among the papers of the treasury. Revised code, page 414.

18

AN ACT

To amend an "Act to establish a College in the Mississippi Territory."
Passed 30th January, 1826.

SECTION 1. *Be it enacted by the Senate and House of Representatives of the State of Mississippi, in General Assembly convened,* That the Governor, and Lieutenant Governor be, and they are hereby constituted ex-officio Trustees of Jefferson College, during their continuance in office. And the Governor for the time being, shall be President of the Board of Trustees.

SEC. 2. *And be it further enacted,* That no vacancy which has occurred, or may occur in the Board of Trustees of said College, by death, resignation or otherwise, shall be filled until the number of Trustees be reduced to twenty-five; and when the number of Trustees shall be so reduced, all vacancies occurring thereafter shall be reported to the General Assembly, by the President of the Board in his annual report, whereupon the General Assembly shall proceed to fill such vacancy by joint vote of both houses, if they deem the interests of the institution to require it, otherwise to direct the Board of Trustees to fill such vacancy, in the manner provided by the act to which this is an amendment: *Provided,* That such vacancies be filled at the stated meetings of the Board.

SEC. 3. *And be it further enacted,* That hereafter there shall be two stated meetings of the Board of Trustees in each and every year, to wit: on the second Monday in January, and first Monday in July. And it shall be the duty of the persons enumerated in the first section of this act, to attend at least one stated meeting in each year.

SEC. 4. All acts conflicting with the foregoing are repealed.

See Acts of the 10th Session of the General Assembly, Chap. XL.

AN ACT

Concerning Jefferson College. Passed 25th December, 1833.

SECTION 1. *Be it enacted by the Legislature of the State of Mississippi,* That the Board of Trustees of Jefferson College be, and they are hereby empowered and directed to fill all vacancies in said Board, which exist at the time of the passage of this act, or which may hereafter exist until the third Monday in January, eighteen hundred and thirty-six, by an election to be made by the Board of Trustees.

SEC. 2. *And be it further enacted,* That this act shall take effect and be in force from and after the passage thereof.

See Acts of the 17th Session of the General Assembly, Chapter
XXIII.

CATALOGUE
OF THE OFFICERS OF THE BOARD OF TRUSTEES,
WITH DATE OF ELECTION, AND TERM OF SERVICE.

PRESIDENTS.

Gov. WM. C. C. CLAIBORNE, From 3d January, 1803, to 11th May, 1805.
"   ROBERT WILLIAMS,   " 11th May, 1805, to 27th August, 1810.
"   DAVID HOLMES,   " 27th August, 1810, to 19th Feb'y, 1820.
BEVERLY R. GRAYSON,   " 19th Feb'y, 1820, to 29th April, 1820.
WILLIAM B. SHIELDS,   " 29th April, 1820, to 18th April, 1823.
BEVERLY R. GRAYSON,   " 12th July, 1823, to 30th January, 1826.
Gov. DAVID HOLMES,   " 30th January, 1826, (Ex-officio.)
GERARD C. BRANDON,
ABRAM M. SCOTT,
H. G. RUNNELS,   }   Ex-officio during their incumbency as Governors of the State.
CHARLES LYNCH,
A. G. McNUTT,

VICE PRESIDENTS.

WILLIAM DUNBAR,   From 3d January, 1803, to 5th May, 1810.
DAVID HOLMES,   " 5th May, 1810, to 27th August, 1810.
COWLES MEAD,   " 27th August, 1810, to 5th M y, 1827.
B. R. GRAYSON,   " 5th M y, 1827, to 7th July, 1834.
WHITE TURPIN,   " 7th July, 1834, to 29th March, 1838.
JOHN A. QUITMAN,   " 29th March, 1838, to 22d April, 1839.
JOHN T. GRIFFITH,   " 22d April, 1839, (present incumbent.)

SECRETARIES.

FELIX HUGHES,   From 3d January, 1803, to 5th May, 1810.
JAMES SMYLIE,   " 5th May, 1810, to 22d December, 1810.
WHITE TURPIN,   " 1st January, 1811, to 13th August, 1813.
HENRY TOOLEY,   " 13th August, 1813, to 20th Dec. 1816.
B. R. GRAYSON,   " 20th Dec., 1816, to 19th Feb'y, 1820
LOUIS WINSTON,   " 19th February, 1820, to 19th Aug. 1820.
JOSEPH DUNBAR,   " 9th Sept. 1820, to 11th Nov., 1824.
LEVIN WAILES,   " 11th Nov., 1824, (present incumbent.)

TREASURERS.

ALEX'R MONTGOMERY, From 6th June, 1803, to
PARKE WALTON,   " 20th Feb'y, 1812, to 27th April, 1814.
NEHEMIAH TILTON,   " 27th April, 1814, to
HENRY TOOLEY,   " 25th Oct., 1814, to 1st March, 1817.
WHITE TURPIN,   " 1st March, 1817, to 9th January, 1837.
B. L. C. WAILES,   " 9th Jan'y, 1837, (present incumbent.)

LIBRARIANS.

B. L. C. WAILES,   From 4th April, 1829, to 7th June, 1836.
THORNTON W. CLAPP,   " 7th June, 1836, to 15th Nov'r, 1836.
J. W. MONETTE.   " 9th Jan'y, 1837, to 11th March, 1837,
CALEB G. FORSHEY,   " 11th March, 1837, to 11th March, 1838.
LEVIN WAILES,   " 9th April, 1838, to 1st May, 1839.
WILLIAM WHIELDON,   " 1st May, 1839, (present incumbent.)

PRESENT BOARD OF TRUSTEES,

WITH THE DATE OF THE ELECTION OF EACH MEMBER.

CATALOGUE

EMBRACING ALL THE TRUSTEES ELECTED,

FROM THE DATE OF THE CHARTER TO THE PRESENT TIME, IN THE ORDER OF THEIR APPOINTMENT.

1. Wm. C. C. Claiborne, 1802.
2. Anthony Hutchins, "
3. William Dunbar, "
4. Benjamin Farrar, "
5. William Vousden, "
6. John Ellis, "
7. David Kerr, "
8. Adam Bingaman, "
9. David Latimore, "
10. Bernard Lintot, "
11. Cato West, "
12. John Girault, "
13. Thomas M. Green, "
14. Samuel Gibson, "
15. Daniel Burnet, "
16. Felix Hughes, "
17. Alexander Montgomery, "
18. Drury W. Brazeale, "
19. Thomas Calvit, "
20. James Caller, "
21. Nathaniel Christmass, "
22. John Steel, "
23. Abner Green, "
24. Sutton Bankes, "
25. Abram Ellis, "
26. Richard Butler, "
27. Robert Dunbar, "
28. John McGrew, "
29. Jacob Stampley, "
30. Joseph Pannill. "
31. Isaac Gailliard, 1802.
32. John Bisland, "
33. Abram Green, "
34. James Hoggatt, "
35. Zachariah Kirkland, 1803.
36. John Hopkins, "
37. Adam Tooley, "
38. David Cooper, "
39. Jas. Nelson, "
40. Isaac Briggs, "
41. John Shaw, 1804.
42. Robert Williams, 1805.
43. Seth Lewis, "
44. Thomas H. Williams, "
45. Philander Smith, "
46. John Cox, 1810.
47. David Holmes, "
48. David Greenleaf, "
49. Everard Green, "
50. James Smylie, "
51. Ferdinand L. Claiborne, "
52. Cowles Mead, "
53. John Wood, "
54. Silas Dinsmoor, "
55. William B. Shields, "
56. Robert Cox, "
57. White Turpin, "
58. Daniel Rawlings, "
59. Wm. Gordon Forman, "
60. James Kempe, 1811.

61. Henry Daingerfield, 1811.
62. Thomas Freeman, "
63. Walter Leake, "
64. Thomas Hinds, "
65. Ralph Regan, "
66. Nehemiah Tilton, "
67. Burwell Vick, "
63. Park Walton, "
69. Gerard C. Brandon, 1812.
70. Andrew H. Holmes, "
71. Josiah Simpson, "
72. Joseph Carson, "
73. George Poindexter, "
74. Edward Turner, "
75. Nathaniel A. Ware, "
76 Christopher Rankin, "
77. John W. Walker, "
78. Zeno Orso, "
79. Henry Tooley, 1813.
80. Francis Gillart, "
81. Charles Blanchard, "
82. Samuel Brown, 1814.
83. Egbert Jansen, "
84. Charles M Norton, "
85. Alexander Covington, "
86. Samuel L. Winston, "
87. Joseph Dunbar, 1816.
88. Beverly R. Grayson, "
89. Archibald Lewis, "
90. Peter Bisland, 1817.
91. Clement Nash Read, "
92. Joseph Forman, "
93. Samuel Brooks, "
94. Lewis Evans, "
95. James McAllister, "
96. John W. Bryan, "
97. Hugh Stanard, "
98. George Newman, 1818.
99. Lyman Harding, 1819.
100. Samuel Postlethwaite, "
101. Nathaniel Hoggatt, "
102. James Hewett, "
103. Lewis Winston, "
104. Charles B. Green, "
105. Joseph Bullen, "
106. James G. Wood, "

107. Andrew Macrerey, 1820.
108. Gamaliel Pease, "
109. R. F. N. Smith, "
110. Adam L. Bingaman, "
111. John McCabb, "
112. Jonathan Thompson, "
113. Thomas B. Reed, "
114. William Wier, 1821.
115. John Snodgrass, "
116. James T. Magruder, Sen. "
117. Samuel Monette, "
118. William L. Chew, 1822.
119. Joseph Sessions, 1823.
120. James Smith, "
121. Levin Wailes, "
122. Robert Andrews, "
123. R. R. Randolph, "
124. Richard E. Mead, 1824.
125. Samuel Dunbar, "
126. Alexander Young, "
127. William B. Melvin, "
128. B. L. C. Wailes, "
129. John C. Burruss, "
130. George C. Ferguson, 1825.
131. Samuel Hunter, "
132. James Pilmore, "
133. William Lemon, "
134. Thomas Freeland, "
135. Stephen Duncan, 1830.
136. William Bisland, "
137. William Stanton, "
138. J. W. Menette, "
139. Philip Hoggatt, 1834.
140. F. L. Claiborne, "
141. James McCaleb, "
142. Levin Covington, "
143. Thomas Farrar, "
144. Richard S. Williams, "
145. John A. Quitman, 1835.
146. William C. Connor, "
147. H. N Smith, "
148. G. L. C. Davis, "
149. John T. McMurran, "
150. Alex'r Montgomery, 1839.
151. John T. Griffith, "

CATALOGUE

OF THE

LIBRARY

OF

JEFFERSON COLLEGE.

The Library comprises fifteen hundred and twenty-two volumes, and will have a continual accumulation of periodical literature, from Europe and America, all of the most popular works of that kind being subscribed for. There is besides a fund of two thousand dollars per annum devoted to its increase. The works marked in the Catalogue with the asterisk are donations.

HISTORY, 149 volumes.

	Vols.		Vols.
Writings of Washington,	9	Modern Europe, by Russell,	
Graham's United States,	2	continued by Jones,	3
Pitkin's United States,	2	Hume's History of England,	
Gordon's History of America,	4	with Smollett's Continuation,	4
New England Chronology,	1	Tytler's Universal History,	2
Winthrop's New England,	2	McIntosh's Revolution,	1
Williamson's Maine,	2	Smith's Thucydides, or History	
Williamson's Vermont,	2	of the Peloponesian Wars,	2
Trumbull's Connecticut,	2	Watson's Reign of Philip II.,	
Belknap's New Hampshire,	1	of Spain,	2
Bradford's Massachusetts,	3	Baker's Livy,	2
Smith's New York,	1	Mills' History of the Crusades,	1
Gazetteer and History of New		Mills' History of Chivalry,	1
Jersey,	1	Scott's History of Scotland,	2

Gordon's Pennsylvania,	1	Crowe's History of France,	3
Proud's Pennsylvania,	2	History of the Netherlands,	1
Bozman's Maryland,	1	History of Switzerland,	1
Smith's Virginia, from the London edition of 1629,	1	His ory of Poland,	1
		History of the Hindoos,	2
Williamson's North Carolina,	2	Rollin's Ancient History,	8
Ramsay's South Carolina,	2	*Rollin's Ancient History, (broken set,)	6
Marshall's Kentucky,	2		
Stoddart's Louisiana,	1	*Washington's Letters, (incomplete,)	2
Martin's Louisiana,	2		
Robertson's Works,	3	Gordon's History of America,	3
Murphy's Tacitus,	1	*Gibbon's Rome, (work incomplete,)	6
Bogue & Bennett's History of Dissenters,	2		
		*Dow's Hindostan,	3
Gordon's Greek Revolution,	2	*History of Mexico,	3
Mitford's Greece,	8	*History of the British Empire, by Plowden,	2
Potter's Antiquities of Greece,	2		
Leland's Ireland,	3	*History of America, by Robertson,	2
Clarendon's History of the Rebellion,	6		
		Dunlop's Roman Literature,	2
Wheaton's History of the North Men,	1	*Tannehill's Sketches of History,	1
Ferguson's Rome,	1	*French Wars, large, with plates,	2
Neibuhr's Rome,	2		
Gibbon's Rome,	4	*Sketches of Russia,	1

BIOGRAPHY, 88 volumes.

Marshall's Life of Washington, with a map,	2	Life of Leo X.,	4
		Life of Lorenzo de Medici,	2
Life of Bishop Heber,	2	Las Cassas' Journal,	4
Southey's Life of Wesley,	2	Life of Ledyard,	1
Life of Sir E. Bridges,	2	Fox's History of James II.,	1
Walton's Lives,	1	Johnson's Life of Greene,	2
Memoirs of Napoleon,	7	Watson's Philip II.,	1
Memoirs of Cardinal de Retz,	3	*Robertson's Charles V.,	2
Memoirs of Pepys,	5	*Watson's Philip III., of Spain,	1
Memoirs of Evelyn,	5	*Boswell's Life of Johnson,	2
Lives of the Norths,	3	*Smellie's Lives,	1
Memoirs of Madam Genlis,	1	*Life of Washington, by Marshall,	4
Life of Elbridge Gerry,	2		
Life of Arthur Lee,	2	*Life of Lorenzo de Medici, by Roscoe,	3
Sparks' Life of Governeur Morris,	3		
		Middleton's Cicero,	2
Life of John Jay,	2	*Life of Addison,	1
Life of Josiah Quincy, Jr.,	1	*Las Cassas' Journal,	1

Life of James Otis,	1	*Memoirs of Lafayette,	1
Sparks' American Biography,	4	*Memoirs of Alexander of Russia,	1
Life of Curran,	1		
Iviney's Life of Milton,	1	*Memoirs of Sir Joshua Reynolds,	1
Life of E. D. Clark,	1		
Life of William Penn,	2		

TRAVELS AND VOYAGES, 69 volumes.

Dwight's Travels,	4	*Young's Travels in France,	2
Denham and Clapperton's Travels,	2	*Clarke's Travels in Europe, Asia and Africa,	1
Dubois' Journal to India,	2	*Bruce's Travels, (odd volume,)	1
Boswell's Tour,	1	*Travels in Sweden, Finland, &c., by Acerbi,	2
McKinney's Tour,	1		
Modern Traveler by Conder,	30	*Staunton's Embassy to China,	1
*Mavor's Voyages, (broken set,)	10	*Bartram's Travels,	1
*Barrow's Travels in China,	1	*Evans' Tour,	1
*Vancouver's Voyages round the World,	6	*Amherst's Embassy to China,	1
		* Moor's Travels,	2

ENGLISH LITERATURE AND CLASSICS, 60 volumes.

Johnson's Works,	6	Milton's Prose and Poetical Works, 4to,	1
Parr's Works,	8	Johnson's Dictionary,	2
Dryden's Prose Works,	4	Edgeworth on Professional Education,	1
Specimens of Early English Poetry,	3	*Spectator,	7
Spectator,	12	*British Classics,	2
Guardian,	3	Hazlitt's Lectures on English Comic Writers,	1
Observer,	3		
Blair's Lectures,	1	*Blair's Lectures, (1st volume,)	1
Same, (abridged edition,)	1	*Blair's Lectures, (abridged,)	1
Campbell's Rhetoric,	1	Harris' Hermes,	1
Lempriere's Classical Dictionary,	1		

PHILOSOPHY, 74 volumes.

Bacon's Works,	10	Observations on Man, by Hartley,	1
Paley's Works,	6		
Brown's Philosophy,	2	Barton's Works of St. Pierre,	1
Tucker's Light of Nature,	4	*Franklin's Works,	1
Stewart's Works,	7	*Stewart's Philosophy of the Human Mind,	1
Locke's Works,	10		

Reed's Essays,	1	*Philosophical Magazine, (incomplete,)	15
Hume's Essays,	2	*Rumford's Philosophical Papers,	1
Cambridge Natural Philosophy,	4	*Rumford's Essays,	3
Fischer's Philosophy,	1	*Nicholson's Philosophy,	2
Cousin's Philosophy,	1		

POETICAL AND DRAMATIC WORKS, 80 volumes.

Warton's Pope,	9	Ossian's Poems,	1
Milton's Works,	2	Shakspeare,	6
British Poets,	50	*Burns' Works, with an account of his life,	4
Ramsay's Poems,	2		
Butler's Works,	2	*Metrical Miscellany, collection of poems by various authors,	1
Johanna Baillie's Poetical Works,	1	*Shakspeare's Dramatic Works, (odd volume,)	1
Mrs. Hemans' Poems,	1		

LATIN AND GREEK WORKS, 117 volumes.

Hederici Lexicon,	1	Homeri Hymni,	1
Dammi's Lexicon,	2	Longini,	1
Oratores Attici,	16	Opera Quinctiliane,	4
Drakenbrock's Livy,	4	Sophocles Tragœdiæ,	1
Xenophon's Works,	7	Brunck's Aristophæ,	4
Poems Lucretius,	1	Bos Elepses Græcæ,	1
Platonis Opera,	8	Greek Gradus,	1
Opera Aristotelis,	8	Lexicon Græco Latinum, folio,	1
Operi Taciti,	4	Homiliarus Doctorum, do.	1
Heyn's Virgil,	4	L. Bonaventuræ Sermones, in 1496, folio,	2
Operi Ovidii,	3		
Butler's Æschylus,	8	Leverett's Latin Lexicon,	1
Theocritus,	2	Heyn's Pindar,	2
Ciceronis Opera,	13	Plutarchi Vitæ,	9
Bentley's Lucan,	1	Homeri Ilias,	1
Ruperti Juvenalis,	1	*Epicteti,	1
Cæsar's Commentaries,	1	Satires of Persius, (translation,)	1

FRENCH WORKS, 131 volumes.

Wilson's French and English Dictionary,	1	Voltaire's Works, Political, Biographical, Poetical, Dramatic, &c.,	91
Dictionaire de l'Academie Francoise,	2	Works of Moliere,	8

Miege's French Dictionary,	1
La Harp's Cours de Literature,	16
French Synonimes,	2
Works of Racine,	7
Works of Boleau Despraux,	3

PERIODICAL AND MISCELLANEOUS, 282 volumes.

American Encyclopædia	13
Drake's Gleaner,	4
North American Review, and Index,	41
Edinburgh Review,	59
Elgin Marbles,	2
Connoisseur,	2
Quarrels of Authors,	2
Walpole's Letters,	2
Collingwood's Correspondence,	1
Heckewelder's Narratives,	1
Jefferson's Notes on Virginia,	1
D gerando on Education,	1
Jefferson's Works,	4
*Do. in board,	4
Lee's Campaigns of 1781,	1
Gibbon's Miscellaneous Works,	2
Annual Register, with Index,	89
Franklin's Works,	1
Irving's Works,	1
Instruction of Boys,	1
*Smollett's Miscellaneous Works, (only the 1st & 3d of 6 volumes,	2
*Pamphlets on Political and other subjects, (bound in 1 volume,)	1
*London Monthly Review, from Jan. 1800 to Dec. 1804,	15
*Edinburgh Review,	13
Domestic Encyclopædia,	2
Temple's Works, in 4 volumes,	4
Goldsmith's Works,	1
*Literary Gazette,	1
*Port Folio,	1
*Analectic Magazine,	2
*Harriet's Struggles,	1
*Hobhouse's Illustrations of Childe Harold,	1
*Lady Morgan's France,	1
*Ten Years' Exile of Madam de Stael,	1
*Rodolph, by Benjamin Constant,	1
*Saturday Magazine,	2
*North American Review,	1
*Edinburgh Review, (14 numbers,)	

POLITICAL, 17 volumes.

Webster's Speeches,	2
Federalist,	1
Virginia Convention, 1829 and 1830,	1
Hallam's Constitutional History,	3
	3
Burke's Works,	3
Say's Political Economy,	1
Rae's Political Economy,	1
Coleridge's Political Works,	3
American Constitutions,	1
*Smith's Wealth of Nations,	17

GEOGRAPHICAL AND STATISTICAL, 37 volumes.

Danville's Ancient Geography,	2
Malte Brun's Geography,	6
Flint's Geography Western States,	1
Catalogue of Harvard College Library,	2
Holmes' Annals,	2
*Humboldt's New Spain,	2
*Census United States 1790 to 1830,	1
*Statistics of Scotland,	20
*Guthrie's Grammar,	1

ARTS AND SCIENCES, 78 volumes.

Elements of Technology,	1
Rose's Chemistry,	1
Lacroix Elementary Treatise on Arithmetic,	1
Cambridge Mathematics,	2
Jacob on Precious Metals,	1
Spurzheim's Phrenology,	1
Nuttall's Ornithology,	2
Newton's Principia,	
Mecanique Celeste De La Place, translated into English, with commentaries, by Nathaniel Bowditch, 3 large folio volumes, with plates,	3
Wilson's Ornithology, with plates,	2
*Repertory of Arts,	9
*Miller's Retrospect,	1
*Barton's Botany,	*
*Ferguson's Astronomy,	2
Silliman's Journal,	7
*Transactions of the American Philosophical Society,	5
Farraday's Chemical Manipulations,	1
Gales' Elements of Chemistry,	1
*Goldsmith's Animated Nature,	4
Couvier's Animal Kingdom,	4
*Vince's Astronomy,	2
*Pennant's Outlines,	4
*Medical Repository,	4
*Harlam's Fauna Americana,	1
*Manual of Hebrew and English Lexicon,	1
*Steward's Hebrew Grammar,	1
*French and English Dictionary,	1
*Handmaid to the Arts,	2
Anderson's Commerce,	6
*Commercial Dictionary, (2d and 3d volumes.)	2
Lawrence's Physiology,	1

THEOLOGY AND ETHICS, 24 volumes.

Knox's Works, Moral and Literary Essays, Epistles, and Sermons,	7
John's Biblican Archeology,	1
Mosheim's Ecclesiastical History,	4
Robinsons Calmet's Dictionary of the Holy Bible,	1
Godwin on Atheism,	1
Berkley's Works,	3
*Orations of the Emperor Julian,	1
*Biblia Hebraica,	1
*Vetus Testamentum Græcum,	1
*Novum Testamentum Græcum,	1
*Biblia Sacra, versio vulgata,	1
*La Sainte Bible,	1
*Biblia Sagrada,	1

LAW AND GOVERNMENT, 20 volumes.

Vattel's Law of Nations,	1
Sidney on Government,	3
Montesquieu's Spirit of Laws,	2
Burlemaque Political Law,	2
Blackstone's Commentaries,	4
Jacobs' Law Dictionary,	6
Puffendorff's Law of Nature and Nations, folio,	1
*Vattel's Law of Nations,	1

AGRICULTURE AND HORTICULTURE, 11 volumes.

*Marshall's Gardening,	1	*American Husbandry,	2
*Marshall's Rural Economy,	2	*Forsyth on Fruit Trees,	1
*Agricultural Transactions,	1	*McMahon's Gardening,	1
*Farmer's Dictionary,	1	*Carey's Address, ,	1
*Gleanings of Husbandry,	1		

DONATIONS FROM CONGRESS, 285 volumes.

Journal of the Federal Convention in Philadelphia for forming the Constitution, from May 14 to Sept. 17, 1787,	1	Pitkin's Statistics,	1
		Statistical Tables,	1
		Fifth Census United States,	1
Journals of the House of Representatives,	23	Gales & Seaton's American State Papers, (large folio volumes, viz:	
Senate Journals,	14	Foreign Relations,	4
Diplomatic Correspondence,	19	Finance,	3
Senate Documents,	57	Public Lands,	3
State Papers,	75	Military Affairs,	2
Executive Documents,	31	Indian Affairs,	
Reports of Committees, &c.	33	Naval Affairs,	⎫ 21
American Archives, (folio,)	1	Commerce and Navigation,	2
Secret Journals of Congress,	5	Post Office,	1
Seybert's Statistics, (folio,)	1	Claims,	1
Gordon's Digest Laws U. S.	1	Miscellaneous,	2

GENERAL

REGULATIONS AND PROVISIONS

FOR THE GOVERNMENT OF

JEFFERSON COLLEGE.

ART. 1. The College, and inferior schools attached thereto, are under the mediate control of the Board of Trustees, and immediately of the President, Professors, and Instructors.

ART. 2. The authority of the Board of Trustees is supreme, in enacting laws for the preservation of order, the promotion of sound morality, the advancement of learning, and the general prosperity of the institution. They appoint and remove all officers and teachers, in every department, inspect their conduct, correct abuses, determine appeals from the decision of the Faculty, decide on the expulsion of students, whose cases have been referred to them by the Faculty; and conduct the general and fiscal interests of the institution.

ART. 3. The Board shall have four stated meetings in each year, to-wit:

On the Second Monday in January;
On the Second Monday in March;
On the First Monday in July, and
On the First Monday in October;

besides adjourned and called meetings. The attendance of seven members is required to constitute a quorum to transact business.

ART. 4. The Board of Trustees have paramount authority in virtue of their character; and no member of the Faculty holds a seat at their Board.

ART. 5. In virtue of their authority and trust, the Board has a right to call upon the President or any officer of the College, for any information in writing, relative to the existence of real or supposed improprieties, disorders, or neglect in the institution.

Art. 6. The Board of Trustees in the official discharge of their duties, and in their deliberations, are to be governed by strict confidence and a high sense of honor and duty, not to be influenced by favor, fear, or intrigue.

Art. 7. The College shall be open to the admission of youth generally who shall be entitled to its benefits, without distinction.

Art. 8. The Collegiate year is divided into two sessions; the FIRST SESSION commences on the first day of March and ends on the last day of July; the SECOND SESSION commences on the first day of October and ends on the last day of February. There shall be a vacation during the months of August and September, and a recess of two weeks at Christmas, and each session shall be reckoned as one hundred and fifty days in computing tuition charges. The thirty first day of July shall be commencement day, except when the month ends on Sunday, when it shall be the day previous.

Art. 9. The President or Vice President, or the Secretary with the concurrence of two members of the Board, may at any time call a meeting of the Board, by giving twelve days previous notice.

Art. 10. When a quorum fail to attend at any stated, adjourned, or called meeting, three members present may adjourn to any given day, and the Secretary shall give notice of the same to the members.

Art. 11. The Faculty of Jefferson College shall consist of the President and such Professors in the College proper, as the Trustees shall appoint.

Art. 12. The President has paramount authority in the College under the Trustees; he is the Chief Executive of the laws enacted by the Board, for the government of the College; and has the right to regulate, with the advice of the other members of the Faculty, all duties allotted by the Board of Trustees to those under his direction.

Art. 13. The Faculty, of which the President is *ex officio* chairman, have original jurisdiction in all matters of discipline; they may enact and enforce such regulations as they may deem expedient, for the good government of the College, not contrary to those enacted by the Trustees.

VICE PRESIDENT OF BOARD OF TRUSTEES.

Sec. 1. The Vice President is elected by a majority of any Board of the Trustees, whenever the office becomes vacant by death or resignation.

Sec. 2. He performs all the duties of President of the Board, in the absence of the President *ex officio*.

TREASURER.

SEC. 1.   The Treasurer shall be elected annually by ballot at the stated meeting in January, or the first meeting thereafter, at which nine members shall be present : and a vote of two-thirds of those present shall be required to elect him.

SEC. 2.   It is the duty of the Treasurer to be well informed as regards all the provisions, transactions, and pecuniary affairs of the Board, generally and specially.

SEC. 3.   He shall have charge of all the funds, stocks and securities belonging, or pertaining to the College, for safe and advantageous keeping; to invest the principal to the best advantage for the College, as directed by the Board of Trustees; to receive all dividends and other revenues of the College, and pay all demands against the same when directed by the Board; to keep a strict business-like account of all finances and disbursements; and to report the state of the College funds to the Board from time to time.

SEC. 4.   He shall make out semi-annually, and render to the Board, regularly at the close of each session, a detailed written report of all receipts, expenditures, and balances, accompanied with the proper vouchers.

SEC. 5.   He may pay the salaries of the President, Professors, Instructors and Officers, at the close of each quarter, without a special order of the Board; provided they are not in default to the College.

SEC. 6.   As compensation for his time of services as Treasurer, he shall be entitled to receive a salary of three hundred dollars per annum.

SECRETARY.

SEC. 1.   The Secretary shall be elected annually by ballot, and a majority of those present at the election of Treasurer shall be required to elect him: but any Board may elect a Secretary *pro tem.*, or to fill a vacancy for an unexpired term, or until the stated meeting in January.

SEC. 2.   He shall have a stated salary of two hundred and fifty dollars per annum.

SEC. 3.   It is the duty of the Secretary to take charge of all papers, documents and correspondence of the Board: he shall keep a journal, and record the proceedings of the Board; and at the opening of each meeting he shall read the minutes of the last previous meeting, as recorded in his journal; he shall notify all members of any appointed meeting; furnish copies of resolutions under the direction of the Board, and perform such other duties as the Board may require.

LAWS

OF

JEFFERSON COLLEGE.

CHAPTER I.—OFFICERS AND FACULTY.

ARTICLE I.—THE PRESIDENT.

Sec. 1. To him is committed the general superintendence and control in the police and studies of the College, and the Primary School. With the advice and consent of the other members of the Faculty, he may make such rules and regulations, and apportionment of duties, as he may deem best adapted for advancing the interests of the institution, and the students connected with the same.

Sec. 2. He shall personally attend to the admission of all students and pupils into the institution, both in the College proper and in the Primary School, according to the regulations relative to admission.

Sec. 3. He shall keep a book register, in which he shall enter the name, age, studies, progress and deportment of every student; which book or register shall be at all times subject to the inspection of the Board of Trustees.

Sec. 4. When any student or pupil is admitted, he shall refer him to the proper department, according to his proficiency.

Sec. 5. He shall carefully file receipts of the Treasurer and Steward, received from applicants, and deliver them to the Vice President or acting Chairman of the Board of Trustees, at the close of each session.

Sec. 6. He shall see that no student is received into any department contrary to the College laws. Chap. 2d.

Sec. 7. He shall report to the Board, in writing, all injuries of College property; all vacancies of Instructors; all failures of duty in the Instructors and Professors, and all other things within his immediate cognizance, requiring the action of the Trustees.

Sec. 8. Immediately after commencement day of each year, the President shall make out and present to the Board of Trustees, a conduct roll, in which the relative demerit of each student during the previous year shall be represented by appropriate numbers.

Sec. 9. He shall also report the names and grades of five students in each regular class, who have made the greatest proficiency; and in like manner, the names of five students in the modern languages and scientific department of the institution, who have attained the highest distinction in the several studies in which they are engaged, in order that their progress and attainments may appear in the catalogue as an incitement to application, and as an honorable evidence of their standing in the institution.

Sec. 10. He shall cause to be executed by the students in drawing, painting and topography, and laid before the Board for exhibition on commencement day, specimens of their performances, such as topographical plans, architectural and other drawings, and paintings; also, lithographic drawing and printing; and such specimens as possess sufficient merit, shall afterwards be preserved in the College Library.

Sec. 11. In addition to his other duties, he shall hold the Professorship, and exercise the duties of Professor of Moral and Intellectual Philosophy and Belles Lettres, and shall lecture at least once a fortnight.

ARTICLE II.—PROFESSORS.

Sec. 1. It is the duty of each Professor, to be vigilant in detecting and repressing disorders, and punishing offenders, when the case is within the jurisdiction of a single officer, and to report all others to the President. It is their duty to visit the rooms of the students frequently; into which they shall have free access at all times.

Sec. 2. The Professors and Instructors shall perform such duties as shall be assigned them by the President in their proper departments.

Sec. 3. Each Professor and Instructor in the College shall make a weekly report, in writing, to the President, of the progress of his classes; an abstract of which shall be laid before the Board of Trustees, or handed to the Secretary, by the President, once every month.

Sec. 4. Each Professor is bound to perform, or shall be held responsible for the performance of *all the duties pertaining to his Professorship*, without extra compensation.

Sec. 5. Each Professor and Instructor, before entering upon the duties of his appointment, shall subscribe a declaration in presence of the Board of Trustees, acknowledging his responsibilities, and pledging himself for the faithful discharge of his several obligations; which declaration shall be kept by the Trustees.

CHAPTER II.—ADMISSION OF STUDENTS.

Sec. 1. Testimonials, of good moral character and correct habits, will be required of every applicant for admission into College proper; and no one from any other College shall be admitted, unless he produces a certificate of having left such College in honorable standing.

Sec. 2. The matriculation fee is five dollars.

Sec. 3. The charge for tuition, in the College and Primary School, is regulated by the Board of Trustees, but it shall always be moderate.

Sec. 4. Before admission, every applicant is required to produce to the President, the certificate of the Treasurer, acknowledging the receipt of the money required to cover the demands of the College for one session in advance; and also the Steward's receipt for boarding, lodging, &c., for one half session in advance. Any officer, admitting a student without such receipts, shall be held responsible for the amount.

Sec. 5. Every applicant admitted into College, shall, within three days, read the laws of the College and shall sign the following declaration; viz: "Having read the laws for the government of Jefferson College, I promise faithfully and conscientiously to observe them, and submit myself to the instructions and government of the officers of the College, yielding them all proper marks of respect and obedience, so long as I continue a student of the institution:" which is to be kept by the President among the archives of the College.

Sec. 6. Every student admitted into the College, shall be furnished by the President with a copy of the laws, and a certificate of his admission, which every student is bound to preserve on pain of suspension.

. Sec. 8. The President may issue a certificate to the Treasurer, informing him whether an applicant is prepared for College or the Primary School.

CHAPTER III.—COURSE OF INSTRUCTION.

OF THE FULL COURSE.

Sec. 1. Applicants for the Freshman Class must stand an approved examination, in English Grammar; Arithmetic, particularly the Rule of Three, Vulgar and Decimal Fractions, Square and Cube Root; Ancient and Modern Geography; the Grammars of the Latin and Greek Languages; Cæsar's Commentaries; Sallust; six books of the Æneid; Latin Prosody and Mair's Introduction; Greek Reader; Gospels of St. Matthew and St. John; Græca Minora, or Lucian's Dialogues; and three books of Xenophon's Cyropædia.

SECTION II.—STUDIES OF THE FRESHMAN YEAR.

FIRST SESSION.	SECOND SESSION.
Cicero's Select Orations, or Livy.	The Odes of Horace.
Xenophon's Anabasis.	Græca Majora, begun.
Latin Prose Translation.	Roman Antiquities.
Roman Antiquities.	Latin Composition, in verse.
Ancient Geography, reviewed.	Mythology.
Davies' Algebra.	Legendre's Geometry.
French Grammar and Exercises in translation.	French Grammar and Telemachus.

SECTION III.—STUDIES OF THE SOPHOMORE YEAR.

FIRST SESSION.	SECOND SESSION.
Horace's Satires.	Cicero de Officiis.
Iliad of Homer.	Græca Majora.
Greek Antiquities.	Greek and Latin Composition in prose and verse.
Greek Prose Translation.	Greek Antiquities.
Greek Prosody and Metre, with Choral scanning.	Chronology.
Hackley's Trigonometry, plane and spherical, and Navigation.	Davies' Analytical Geometry.
Davies' Surveying.	Davies' Differential and Integral Calculus.
Descriptive Geometry.	Rhetoric, continued.
Blair's Rhetoric.	Lectures on English Literature.
French Grammar, and Voltaire's Life of Charles XII.	Works of Racine or Corneille.

SECTION IV.—STUDIES OF THE JUNIOR YEAR.

FIRST SESSION.	SECOND SESSION.
Cicero de Oratore, and Horace's Epistles.	Cicero de Natura Deorum, or Lucretius.
Alcestis of Euripides.	Euripides' Medea.
Plato's Phædo and Crito, from Græca Majora.	Œdipus Tyranus of Sophocles.
Lectures on the Roman Language and Literature.	Lectures on Greek Literature.
Mechanics.	Mechanics, completed.
Electricity, Magnetism, and Electro-Magnetism.	Whateley's and Campbell's Philosophy of Rhetoric.
Chemistry.	Kames' Elements of Criticism.
Whateley's Logic.	Say's Political Economy.
Evidences of Revealed Religion.	Finance.
Montesquieu's Esprit des Lois.	Montesquieu or Montaigne.

SECTION V.—STUDIES OF THE SENIOR YEAR.

FIRST SESSION.	SECOND SESSION.
Prometheus Vinctus of Æschylus; and	Longinus on the Sublime, or Aristotle's Treatise on Rhetoric.
Demosthenes' Select Orations.	Lectures on Philology.
Tacitus.	Mineralogy.
Lectures on Greek Literature.	Geology.
Optics.	Natural History.
Astronomy.	Ethics.
Chemistry, applied to the Arts.	International and Constitutional Law.
Political Economy, completed.	Lectures on Modern History and Literature, and the Fine Arts.
Cousin's Elements of Psychology.	Works of Boileau.
Works of Moliere.	

CHAPTER IV.—OF THE PARTIAL, OR ENGLISH AND SCIENTIFIC COURSE.

SEC. 1.   Students applying for admission into the Partial Course, must be thoroughly acquainted with Arithmetic, viz: the four *ground* rules, Simple and Compound Reduction, Single Rule of Three, Vulgar and Decimal Fractions, and Square and Cube Root.

SEC. 2.   For admission into the Class of Engineering, a thorough knowledge of the above prescribed Course of Mathematics and Mechanics, will be required.

SEC. 3.   For admission to the Course of Belles Lettres and Intellectual Philosophy, or the Modern Languages, a good knowledge of English Grammar and Parsing, with the ability to write the English Language correctly, will be required.

Sec. 4. Instruction shall be given, to such students as desire it, in the French, Spanish and German Languages, and in Drawing and Painting; also, in a complete course of Commercial Education, comprehending Book-keeping and Mercantile Law.

Sec. 5. Students desirous of pursuing any branch of Liberal Education, with a view to their future destination or pursuits, may, without being required to conform to the regular College course, be admitted to the College proper, and the President shall assign them such studies, and attach them to such classes, as will be best calculated to promote their views.

Sec. 6. Students in Mathematics and Civil Engineering, shall be instructed in the use of the appropriate instruments, and shall be exercised in practical operations in Field and Trigonometrical Surveying, taking heights and distances, leveling, &c.

Sec. 7. The Military Science, or Art of War, is not taught in this Institution: but as a popular, pleasing, manly and efficient substitute for gymnastics, the martial exercise, or military drill, is adopted, to occupy, in part, the intervals usually devoted, in literary institutions, to recreation.

CHAPTER V.—DEGREES AND GRADUATION.

Sec. 1. Students having completed the foregoing course, and having sustained a thorough examination in all the branches, shall be considered entitled to the degree of Bachelor of Arts.

Sec. 2. Alumni in pursuit of learning, who shall have maintained a good moral character for three years, after having received the degree of A. B., shall be entitled to a diploma for the degree of Master of Arts, by paying the common graduation fees.

Sec. 3. Students who prosecute particular branches of study, may receive certificates of their degree of proficiency therein, to be written in English, signed by the President, and countersigned by the Secretary of the Board of Trustees, with the seal of the College annexed.

Sec. 4. All Diplomas for degrees, shall be signed by the President and Professors, and countersigned by the President, or Vice President, and Secretary of the Board of Trustees, with the seal of the College affixed.

Sec. 5. The exercises of commencement day are to be regulated by the Faculty.

Sec. 6. The President shall be entitled to a fee of five dollars, from each graduate, for furnishing and executing a Diploma on parchment.

CHAPTER VI.—HOURS OF STUDY, AND APPROPRIA-TION OF TIME.

Sec. 1. The days of study are from Monday to Saturday at noon, inclusive; during which time the hours appropriated to study, are from sunrise in the morning until 10 o'clock at night; excepting the time from breakfast till 9 o'clock, A. M., and from noon until 2 o'clock, P. M., and from 5 o'clock, (in summer from 6,) P. M., until dark.

Sec. 2. All students are required to be diligent in prosecuting the studies respectfully assigned them; and are strictly to confine themselves to their rooms during study hours, except when attending morning or evening prayers, and the recitations of their respective classes.

Sec. 3. No student, without the special permission of the President, shall be allowed to attend upon the instruction of any teacher of any language, art or science, if said teacher be not connected with the College.

Sec. 4. Every student shall perform the duties and exercises assigned to him by the Faculty.

Sec. 5. They are required to attend daily at the recitations of their classes, when and wherever directed.

Sec. 6. Exercises shall be prepared and read frequently by the students before their classes. These shall consist of original composition, and of translations of the Latin, Greek, French, Spanish and German, into English, and *vice versa;* the exercises to be left with the proper Instructors for correction and remards.

Sec. 7. As a relaxation from study, to afford the students a manly and agreeable means of amusement, as well as for the promotion of health, and to invigorate the faculties, mental and physical, a period not exceeding one hour, at the close of each day, shall be devoted to military drill and exercise, under the command and instruction of the Superintendent and officers appointed for that purpose.

Sec. 8. On each Saturday, from 9 o'clock, A. M., to 1, P. M., the exercises shall consist of a public examination on the studies of the past week; of lectures by the President and Professors, illustrated by appropriate experiments in Chemistry and Natural Philosophy; and of declamation by the students. From 1 to 2 o'clock shall be appropriated to a military drill, review and inspection of the students. During the residue of the day there shall be a recess.

Sec. 9. A public examination of all the students, shall be held at the close of each session, on all the branches of their previous studies.

Sec. 10. At each public stated examination, in addition to a Board of Visitors appointed by the Faculty, the Board of Trustees shall appoint from their members, two Committees of Inspection : one for the College proper, and one for the Primary School; whose duty shall be, to attend all the exercises, and observe closely, and report to the Board, their convictions as to the proficiency of the pupils and students, and their previous application; the order and system observed by the Instructors, their discipline, and the manner in which they have acquitted themselves in their general stations ; and any thing else which may present to their observation.

Sec. 11. The President may, at any other time, order the examination of any class or classes, either in public or in private.

Sec. 12. Students who remain in the College during the vacations, are subject to all the laws of the Institution in regard to decorum and moral conduct.

CHAPTER VII.—OBSERVANCE OF THE SABBATH AND RELIGIOUS WORSHIP.

Sec. 1. The students are bound to attend morning and evening prayers by the President, in the College Hall, at stated hours : and to behave with decency and solemnity during the same.

Sec. 2. The students shall attend such religious and moral instruction on Sunday, as the President or Faculty may institute ; but no sectarian doctrines shall be inculcated.

Sec. 3. They shall attend divine service at some place in Washington every Sunday, unless excused by the President : the place of worship to be attended by any student to be selected by his parent or guardian, or, when this is not done, by the student himself, with the sanction of the President. Some member of the College shall be appointed to take charge of those attending at each place, who shall be responsible for their orderly and correct behavior.

Sec. 4. Except when going to Church, or with permission of the President, no student shall leave the College grounds on Sunday.

CHAPTER VIII.—DIET AND LODGING.

Sec. 1. All students of the College, as well as of the Primary School, who do not reside with their parents or guardians, are required to board in commons and lodge in the College edifice, or in the Steward's house.

Sec. 2.   All the Faculty as well as the Instructors in every department, who have not families, are required to board in commons and lodge in the College, unless by special exemption by the Board of Trustees.

Sec. 3.   All students are required to treat the Steward and his family with all proper respect; to observe the rules of decorum and good order during meals, and while going to the commons table and returning.

Sec. 4.   The Steward is bound to provide sufficient good and wholesome food at regular hours; and is under no obligation to provide extra meals for students who do not attend at the stated hours, except in cases of sickness, when they shall have from him all the requisite attention without extra charge.

Sec. 5.   Every boarder is required to pay the Steward for board, &c., in advance, until the close of the session.

Sec. 6.   The charge for boarding, lodging, washing, fuel, lights, &c., will be regulated by the Board of Trustees, from time to time.

Sec. 7.   No student shall have any entertainment of any kind in his room, or visit any tavern or eating house in Washington, without special permission.

Sec. 8.   No student shall employ any servant in the College, other than those employed by the Steward.

Sec. 9.   No student is allowed to go into the refectory, except at regular meals; or to visit the Steward's house without express permission or invitation.

Sec. 10.   Any student who may conceive himself neglected by the Steward, or insufficiently supplied by him with food, fuel, or any thing else, may complain to the President, who shall inquire into the grievance, and if any exist, cause it to be corrected; or he shall report it to the Board in session.

CHAPTER IX.—PRESERVATION OF COLLEGE PROPERTY.

Sec. 1.   All students and others are held responsible for any injury they may cause to the College property.

Sec. 2.   The Faculty shall use all diligence to ascertain how, and by whom, any injury to the same may have been committed, and to report the same to the Board of Trustees at their next meeting, if the trespasser have not repaired the same previously.

Sec. 3.   Injuries done to any part of the College edifice, enclosures, or other property, shall be repaired by the Steward, and double the actual cost of the same shall be charged to the person or persons committing the same; the account for which shall be placed with the Treasurer, and stand as a bar to their admission at the next session, if not paid.

Sec. 4. When such injury has been sustained, and the trespasser is not known, the charge shall be made equally against all the students occupying the room in which it was committed; or against all the students of the College, *pro rata*, when the injury (under the same circumstances) has been committed in public or unoccupied rooms and entries.

Sec. 5. Any student, against whom any charge for damage is made or assessd, shall not be considered as having left the College in honorable standing, if the same remain unpaid at the close of the session.

Sec. 6. As the Faculty have the right of visiting the rooms of all students, at any time, if admission be refused by a student, and the door be broken open by any member of the Faculty to obtain entrance, the expense for repairing the same, shall be charged, as in other cases, to the occupants of said room; or to such person or persons as refused the entrance, as the case may be.

Sec. 7. During the vacations, the Steward shall have special charge over the College building and furniture, and if he shall be absent, he shall commit its safe keeping to some judicious and responsible person.

CHAPTER X.—OF DISCIPLINE AND POLICE.

Sec. 1. In all institutions for the education of youth, discipline is of the first importance; in this it will be parental, kind and liberal; *but firm*, and addressed to the good and honorable feelings of the students.

Sec. 2. The character and conduct of gentlemen must be considered as inseparable from every member of this Institution.

Sec. 3. The discipline and police of this Institution will be military, and will be so conducted as to insure promptitude and regularity in every department.

Sec. 4. The utmost order and neatness must be preserved at all times, by all members of the Institution, both in their rooms and in their personal appearance.

Sec. 5. In addition to his other duties, one of the Professors to be designated by the Trustees, shall act as *Superintendent* of the Institution, shall give the students practical instruction in elementary tactics, and under the direction of the President, shall have the supervision of its internal police.

Sec. 6. It shall be the duty of the Superintendent to visit and inspect from time to time the commons and dormitories, and to see that the duties of the Steward are properly performed; he shall investigate all formal complaints made against the Steward, and when well founded, and the cause be not removed upon his requisition, he shall report the matter to the President to be laid before the Trustees when in session.

Sec. 7. The Superintendent, with the concurrence of the President, shall appoint one of the students, of suitable qualifications, to act under his direction and instruction as Commandant, who shall perform the duties of Adjutant, and act as assistant in the drilling and teaching the military exercise, and such student, whilst performing these duties, shall be entitled to his tuition in the College without charge.

Sec. 8. The Superintendent, in like manner, shall appoint from time to time, in rotation, a suitable number of students of competent qualifications, to act as Captains, Subalterns and non-commissioned officers; the appointments so conferred shall be regarded as honorary distinctions, and be bestowed as rewards of meritorious conduct; the term of appointment shall be for the session.

Sec. 9. A competent number of musicians shall be engaged, and shall be entitled to their board, tuition and uniform clothing free of charge, in consideration of their services in this capacity.

Sec. 10. From considerations of economy, as well as to prevent invidious distinctions, and to produce feelings of equality among the students, a uniform dress is required; this shall consist of a blue coat, military cap, pompon and stock, and blue pantaloons and vest; in summer the pantaloons and vest will be white.

Sec. 11. A commissary will be appointed by the Trustees, whose duty it shall be to supply all articles of clothing, books and stationary required for the use of the students, the prices of which shall be regulated by the Board; every thing which the Superintendent may deem *necessary* for the improvement, health and convenience of the students, may thus be supplied at lower rates than they could be otherwise obtained.

Sec. 12. Students are prohibited from making purchases or trading without the permission of the Superintendent, except with the approbation of the parent or guardian.

Sec. 13. Students are prohibited from leaving the College grounds at any time, except under such regulations as the President and Faculty may from time to time adopt; they are likewise required to remain quietly in their rooms during the hours appropriated to study; the Assistant Superintendent and other officers will make frequent and close inspections of their quarters, examining into the condition of their rooms and appurtenances, books, beds, clothing, &c., and report the result to the Superintendent.

SEC. 14. The students shall make their appearance on parade at sunrise every morning; after being exercised by the officers and answering to the roll, they may be dismissed to their studies until called to breakfast.

SEC. 15. At the appointed signal and at the established hours, the students will all assemble on the College parade, and march in regular order to and from their meals.

SEC. 16. The roll shall be called at least three times every day, and all delinquencies shall be noted and reported to the Superintendent.

CHAPTER XI.—DEPORTMENT.

SEC. 1. Any conduct that would be deemed indecorous in genteel private families, is deemed improper in the College edifice.

SEC. 2. All students of the Institution are required and expected to treat the Trustees and Faculty with every mark of respect, as is justly due them as superior officers.

SEC. 3. Disrespect manifested towards the institutions of religion, as observed by any Christian denomination, the laws of morality, and of the land; the regulations adopted for the government and instruction of the College, or to any person clothed with authority in the Institution; any immodesty or indecency in dress, speech, song or action; any act of profaneness; any act of rude or riotous behavior, of tippling in intoxicating liquors, of quarrelling, abusing, insulting, challenging, or fighting with fellow-students or others; of prevarication or lying, of purloining, of playing at cards or dice, or at any other game, whether for money or other valuable article; any association with persons of publicly bad morals, or with persons under sentence of expulsion, (without leave,) within the bounds of Washington; any combinations for resisting the exercise of authority; refusal to give evidence, when required by the government of the College, or neglecting to attend when summoned by any governing officer of the same, or refusal to grant admission into any of the rooms when sought by any member of the Faculty; visiting of any tavern or other house kept for the sale of liquors or victuals, without leave obtained; attendance upon theatrical entertainments; the commencement of judicial process against any fellow-student or officer of the College, without permission by the

Faculty or Board of Trustees, as the case may be; any general course of extravagance in dress, or general expense, or of dissipation; the practice of any known vice; the keeping of guns, pistols, swords, dirks, or any implement of war other than those furnished for military drill and exercise, within the College edifice, or at any other place, except at their parents' or guardians' houses, with their knowledge and approbation; in short, any act, or course of action, which bespeaks a spirit hostile to good order and good government in the Institution; must be regarded as offences cognizable by any and by all the governors of the College, in their capacities of individual officers, members of the Faculty, and of the Board of Trustees, to be punished in the manner authorized by the laws of the College.

Sec. 4. Every student whose conduct has been such as to meet the approbation of the Faculty, wishing to leave College, shall be entitled to a certificate of his standing from the President.

CHAPTER XII.—OFFENCES AND PUNISHMENTS.

Sec. 1. The punishments of the Institution are wholly of a moral nature; they are admonition, extra study, degradation from their classes, from offices of trust and honor, prohibition from wearing the uniform of the institution, suspension and expulsion.

Sec. 2. Admonition may be given by any governing officer of the College, for any of the minor offences, before his own class; or by the Faculty before the offender's class, before their own body, or before all the students assembled in the hall.

Sec. 3. When extra study, on account of negligence, is insufficient to keep a student equal to his class, he may be degraded by the Faculty to a lower class.

Sec. 4. When a student has made himself a very suspicious, dangerous, or obnoxious member of the Institution, by a course of froward, idle, extravagant, dissipated, refractory, or quarrelsome conduct, and is irreclaimable, so that his connection with the College is not beneficial to himself or creditable to the Institution, he shall be suspended or expelled.

CHAPTER XIII.—EXPULSION.

Sec. 1. When the Faculty decide on the necessity of expelling a student, they are to report through the President, all the circumstances of the case to the Board of Trustees, who, alone have the power of expulsion.

Sec. 2. No expelled student can be restored to the privileges of the College, unless by a vote of two-thirds of the members constituting any meeting of the Board of Trustees, with the concurrence of the Faculty.

SEC. 3. If any student leave the College without permission, in resentment for the infliction of any of the penalties according to the laws of the College, either upon himself or upon a fellow-student, he shall not again enter without the consent of the Faculty, by express vote.

CHAPTER XIV.—THE PRIMARY SCHOOL.

SEC. 1. The Primary School is attached to Jefferson College, for the instruction of those students, who are not prepared for entrance into College, and for educating those who do not desire to enter College.

SEC. 2. The Primary School is under the immediate control of the President, and is governed by a Principal Instructor, and one or more Assistant Instructors.

SEC. 3. The Instructors, at the close of every week, shall make a written report to the President of the condition of their respective classes; the number and name of all absentees; and all improper deportment; which reports are subject to the inspection of the Board, whenever called for.

SEC. 4. There shall be two departments in this School : the *First Department* is taught by the Principal Instructor in all those branches of study requisite to prepare students for College; the *Second Department* is conducted by one or more Assistant Instructors, under the direction of the Principal Instructor, for instruction in the rudiments of reading, writing, arithmetic, geography, and English grammar.

SEC. 5. This being a department of Jefferson College, the requisites for admission are the same, as regards the payment of College dues, &c.

SEC. 6. Punishments shall be of a moral nature principally : however, in children under twelve years, slight corporal punishment may be inflicted; but injudicious and severe infliction of the same will subject the Instructor guilty thereof, to the censure of the Board, or dismission.

SEC. 7. Examinations of the pupils in this department shall take place at the same stated times with those in the College proper; but shall be conducted separately by the Instructors thereof.

SEC. 8. The students in this department are equally responsible for damage of College property, or the infraction of any College law.

SEC. 9. The Principal Instructor shall report to the President, all damages committed in his school, and the person by whom committed.

Sᴇc. 10. The hours of teaching in this department, are from 9 until 12 o'clock, M.—and from 2 until 5 o'clock, P. M., during the months from the first of October, until the last of March;—and from the first of April until the close of the session in August, the hours of teaching shall be from 8 o'clock, A. M. until noon, and from 2 o'clock until 6, P. M. During these hours the Instructors shall be diligently engaged in their school rooms.

CHAPTER XV.—SALARIES AND PERQUISITES.

Sᴇc. 1. The salaries of all the officers shall be paid after the close of each quarter, to-wit: on the first day of January, April, July and October.

Sᴇc. 2. The salaries of the President, Professors, and Instructors, shall be regulated by the Board, from time to time: but no reduction of salary shall be made to take effect during the term of their service in the Institution.

Sᴇc. 3. Any time lost, from any other cause than sickness, by any officer or instructor, shall be deducted in payment of salaries, unless such person procure an acceptable substitute to discharge his duties.

CHAPTER XVI.—LIBRARY AND LIBRARIAN.

Sᴇc. 1. The library is for the use of the students of all the College classes, the Faculty, and the Board of Trustees; and the books are *not* to be used as books of study.

Sᴇc. 2. No person shall be permitted to take or keep out at one time, more than one volume.

Sᴇc. 3. Every book taken out shall be returned within two weeks from the day in which it is taken out.

Sᴇc. 4. Every person receiving a book or books from the library, shall subscribe and leave with the librarian, a receipt for the same, specifying its value; which receipt shall be cancelled if the book be returned in good order, and within the prescribed time.

Sᴇc. 5. All the books, belonging to the library, shall be labelled as property of Jefferson College, and numbered regularly in order, commencing with the largest, and having the value on each attached.

Sᴇc. 6. A Librarian shall be appointed by the Board from time to time, with a small fixed salary; and he may be selected from among the Instructors or students.

Sᴇc. 7. He shall file, with the Secretary of the Board, a receipt acknowledging the number of books, &c., received by him in charge.

Sec. 8. It is the duty of the Librarian to keep the books, &c., in the best order; to keep them labelled and regularly numbered; to keep a catalogue of the works and volumes, with their numbers and value, recorded in a book; to see that all books are regularly returned in good order; to receive and cancel the receipts from those applying for books; to report to the Board at their next meeting, any losses or damage sustained in any book or books, and those who are responsible for the same; and in case of loss or damage, he shall not cancel the receipt given for them.

Sec. 9. The Librarian will be held responsible for double the value of any book (or of the set to which it may belong) which he may loan out to a person not entitled to the use of books from the library, provided such book or books be lost or damaged.

Sec. 10. No maps, charts, engravings or documents, shall be permitted to leave the library rooms.

CHAPTER XVII.—OF GRATUITOUS INSTRUCTION.

Sec. 1. For the purpose of extending the benefits of this Institution to every section of the State, one student from each county shall be educated without charge for tuition.

Sec. 2. In addition to the above, five students, to be taken in rotation from the several counties of the State according to their alphabetical arrangement, shall also receive gratuitous instruction in the College; and their expenses for boarding with the Steward, shall be paid out of the fund of the Institution.

Sec. 3. Beneficiaries shall not be known as such, either to the Professors or students of the Institution; but shall be admitted on a recommendation addressed to the Treasurer of the College by the Judge of Probate and President of the Board of Police of the county of their residence, by whom, in all cases, they are to be selected.

Sec. 4. The recommendation of all applicants for admission, under the provisions of this chapter, shall be in the following form, viz:

——————— County, ———, 18—.
To the Treasurer of Jefferson College:
We, ——————, Judge of Probates, and ——————, President of the Board of Police for the County of ——————, do hereby recommend ——————, a resident of said county, for gratuitous instruction in Jefferson College; the said —————— being of good moral character, and, in our opinion, deserving the benefits offered by the Trustees.

Signed, ——————, *Judge of Probates.*
——————, *President Board of Police.*

REMARKS

ON THE

COURSE OF STUDIES

Engineering, Drawing, and the Spanish and German Languages, have not been enumerated among the branches of study absolutely necessary for obtaining a degree. The most thorough and ample instruction will, however, be given to those who desire to obtain a knowledge of them by the Professors in these departments: and, also, delineations of the human figure, landscape sketches from nature, and topography, with crayon, pencil, pen and colors will be taught by the Professor of Drawing.

These branches may be pursued by any student at his own election, having the sanction of his natural or legal guardian, and that of the Faculty, *provided* they do not interfere with the regular course of study before described.

Declamation, Forensic Disputation and English Composition, will be continued regularly through the Sophomore, Junior and Senior Years.

In the choice of text books for the Department of Philosophy and Belles Lettres, some latitude will be exercised according to the exigencies of the occasion. In those branches, where it will be difficult or impossible to procure suitable text books, lectures will be delivered, and an examination of the class on the last lecture delivered, will be held at each succeeding recitation.

In the Classical Department also, it is not expected that the same portions of the same authors will be invariably read by each class, but such changes in the text books and the portions read, will be made by the Professor, with the approval of the President, as the proficiency and aptitude of the class, and other contingent circumstances may require.

It is most urgently pressed upon those who are preparing students for admission into College, to see that they are *thoroughly acquainted* with the rules of Arithmetic above mentioned, and also with Latin and

Greek Grammar, and *Latin Prosody.*   An early attention to this course, would save the pupil an amount of vexation, difficulty and disappointment in his subsequent College course, which none can appreciate, but those who have been the unfortunate subjects of defective instruction, or have been subjected to the unhappy and unenviable drudgery of striving to impart knowledge which the student can neither appreciate nor understand—in other words, of erecting a superstructure where no foundation has been laid.   If all applicants for the Freshman Class, were *thoroughly grounded* in Arithmetic, Latin and Greek Grammar, and particularly *Prosody,* the whole College course. would, with ordinary diligence, be comparatively easy and delightful. But without these indispensable requisites, neither application on the part of the student, nor the genius, ability, and patient industry of the Professor, will avail to relieve the student from embarrassment, disappointment, and eventually disgust.

JEFFERSON COLLEGE,

COURSE OF STUDIES AND EMPLOYMENT

From dawn of day to sunrise.	Sunrise to 7, A. M.	7 to 9 A. M.	9 to 10, A. M.	10 to 11, A. M.	11 to 12, A. M.
Reveille at dawn of day—Roll-call after Reveille—Prayers after Roll-call—Inspection of Rooms 30 minutes after Prayers.		Breakfast at 7—Recreation till 8, A. M.—Studies till 9, A. M.			
	SENIOR				
	*Recitation in Mineralogy, Geology, Political Economy and French.		Recitation in Ancient Languages.	Studies of Psychology, Philology, International and Constitutional Law, Evidences of Revealed Religion.	Recitation in Psychology, Philology, International and Constitutional Law, Evidences of Revealed Religion.
	JUNIOR				
	Recitation in Mechanics.		Study of Ancient Languages and Chemistry.	Study of Electricity, Magnetism, Electro-Magnetism.	Recitation in Ancient Languages, Chemistry, Electricity, Magnetism, Electro-Magnetism.
	SOPHOMORE				
	Study of Mathematics.		Recitation in Trigonometry, Descriptive and Analytical Geometry, Differential and Integral Calculus.	Study of French.	Recitation in French.
	FRESHMAN				
	Recitation in Greek, Latin.		Study of French.	Recitation in French.	Study of Latin and Greek, Composition in Prose and Verse.

*It will be observed, that of the above specified subjects, all will not be recited at the same hour of every day; but that the different days of the week will be occupied with different studies, viz: on Monday, at 7 o'clock, A. M., *Mineralogy;* Tuesday, *Geology;* Wednesday, *Political Economy;* Thursday, *French,* &c.

WASHINGTON, MISS.

OF TIME DURING THE DAY.

12 to 2, P. M.	2 to 3, P. M.	3 to 4. P. M.	4 to 5, P. M.	5 to 6	6 to 8	8 P. M.	10 P. M.
Dinner at 1, P. M.—Recreation till 2, P. M.	**CLASS.**			Roll-call—Prayers—Military Exercises—Dress Parade.	Supper—Recreation till 8, P. M.	Signal to retire to Quarters—Studies till 10, P. M.	Signal to extinguish Lights—Inspection of Rooms.
	Studies of Modern History, Literature and the Fine Arts. Ethics.	Recitation in Modern History, Literature and the Fine Arts, Ethics.	Optics, Astronomy, Chemistry applied to the Arts.				
	CLASS.						
	Study of Logic, Philosophy, French, and Political Economy.	Recitation in Logic, Experimental Philosophy, French and Political Economy, Finance.	Study of Mechanics, Philosophy of Rhetoric and Elements of Criticism.				
	CLASS.						
	Lectures on English Literature, Rhetoric.	Study of Latin, Greek.	Recitation in Latin, Greek.				
	CLASS.						
	Study of Mathematics.	Recitation in Mathematics.	Ancient Mythology, Study of Roman Antiquities.				

ACTS OF CONGRESS

RELATING TO

JEFFERSON COLLEGE.

Extract from the Twelfth Section of the Act of Congress, passed
3d March, 1803, entitled

AN ACT

Regulating the grants of land, and providing for the disposal of the
lands of the United States, South of the State of Tennessee.

Sec 12.   That all the lands aforesaid, not otherwise disposed of
or excepted by virtue of the preceding sections of this act, shall, with
the exception of the section number sixteen, which shall be reserved in
each Township for the support of Schools within the same, *with the
exception also of thirty-six sections to be located in one body by the
Secretary of the Treasury for the use of Jefferson College ; and also
with the exception of such Town lots not exceeding two, in the Town
of Natchez, and of such an out lot adjoining the same, not exceeding
thirty acres, to be located by the Governor of the Mississippi Territory, for the use of said College, be offered for sale, &c. &c.*
(See Revised Code, page 511.)

AN ACT

Authorizing the Secretary of the Treasury to locate the lands reserved
for the use of Jefferson College, in the Mississippi Territory, passed
February 20, 1812.

Sec. 1.   *Be it enacted by the Senate and House of Representatives
of the United States of America, in Congress Assembled,* That the
Secretary of the Treasury be, and he is hereby, authorized and empowered to locate, in one body, the thirty-six sections of land reserved
for the use of Jefferson College in the Mississippi Territory, by an act,
entitled "An Act regulating the grants of land, and providing for the
sale of the lands of the United States, South of the State of Tennessee,"
passed on the third day of March, one thousand eight hundred and
three, on any lands within the said Territory, not sold, or otherwise
disposed of, and to which the Indian title has been extinguished.
Revised Code, page 536.)

D

LOCATION OF LOTS IN THE CITY OF NATCHEZ.

MISSISSIPPI TERRITORY, }
Adams County. }

In pursuance of a law of the United States, entitled "An Act regulating the grants of land, and providing for the disposal of the lands of the United States, South of the State of Tennessee, passed March 3, 1803":

I, WILLIAM C. C. CLAIBORNE, Governor of the Mississippi Territory, do hereby locate a lot of land, situate, lying and being in the Town or City of Natchez, on which stands the house formerly cccupied by the Priests of that place, and in which the Courts of Justice, for the District and County of Adams, are now holden; and also the lot adjoining the before mentioned lot, for the use of Jefferson College, being part of the donation by Congress, as provided in and by the aforesaid act. WILLIAM C. C. CLAIBORNE.

December 2, 1803.

To ISAAC BRIGGS, Esquire, Surveyor of the Lands of the United States, South of the State of Tennessee.

I, HENRY DAINGERFIELD, Secretary of the Mississippi Territory, do hereby certify, that the foregoing is a true and correct transcript of Executive proceedings filed in my office.

In testimony whereof, I have hereunto subscribed my name, and [SEAL.] affixed the seal of my office, at the Town of Washington, this 14th day of September, 1813.

HENRY DAINGERFIELD.

LOCATION OF OUT LOT ADJOINING THE CITY OF NATCHEZ.

To ISAAC BRIGGS, Esquire, Surveyor of the Lands of the United States, South of the State of Tennessee:

MISSISSIPPI TERRITORY.

In pursuance of the Twelfth Section of the law of the United States, entitled "An Act regulating the grants of land and providing for the disposal of the lands of the United States, South of the State of Tennessee":

I, CATO WEST, Secretary, exercising the powers, and performing the duties of the Governor of the Mississippi Territory, do hereby locate the donation of an out lot of thirty acres, adjoining the Town (now City) of Natchez, by the act aforesaid, made to Jefferson College, as follows: Beginning at the south end of the front street of said City, and running at right angles with the same westwardly to the highest part of the River Bluff, thence northwardly along said bluff and eastwardly to the front street aforesaid for quantity.

In testimony whereof, I have hereunto set my hand, and the seal [SEAL] of the Territory aforesaid, the 22d day of December, one thousand eight hundred and three.

CATO WEST.

I, HENRY DAINGERFIELD, Secretary of the Mississippi Territory, do hereby certify, that the foregoing is a true and correct transcript from the records of Executive proceedings filed in my office.

In testimony whereof, I have hereunto subscribed my name, and [SEAL. annexed the seal of my office, at the Town of Washington, this 14th day of September, 1813.

HENRY DAINGERFIELD.

NOTE.—See originals among the papers filed in the suit of Jefferson College against the City of Natchez, in the Circuit Court of Adams County, No. 62, April Term, 1816.   Also, see minutes of said court, page 501, &c.

LOCATION OF LAND GRANTED BY CONGRESS.

TREASURY DEPARTMENT.

WHEREAS, by an Act of Congress, passed on the third day of March, one thousand eight hundred and three, entitled "An Act, regulating the grants of land, and providing for the disposal of the lands of the United States, South of the State of Tennessee," thirty six Sections of land to be located in one body, by the Secretary of the Treasury, for the use of Jefferson College, were excepted from the sales of public lands in the Mississippi Territory.

AND WHEREAS, by another Act of Congress, passed on the twentieth day of February, one thousand eight hundred and twelve, entitled "An Act, authorizing the Secretary of the Treasury to locate the lands reserved for the use of Jefferson College, in the Mississippi Territory," the Secretary of the Treasury is specially authorized and empowered to make the said location on any lands within the said Territory, not sold or otherwise disposed of, and to which the Indian title has been extinguished.

Now, therefore, be it known, That I, ALBERT GALLATIN, Secretary of the Treasury, in pursuance of the authority vested in me, as aforesaid, do hereby locate, for the use of Jefferson College, the Sections numbered One, Two, Three, Four, Five, Six, Seven, Eight, Nine, Ten, Eleven, Twelve, Thirteen, Fourteen, Fifteen, Sixteen, Seventeen, Eighteen, Nineteen, Twenty, Twenty-one, Twenty-two, Twenty-three, Twenty-four, Twenty-five, Twenty-six, Twenty-seven, Twenty-eight, Twenty-nine, Thirty, Thirty-one, Thirty-two, Thirty-three, and Thirty-six, in Township numbered Ten in the Second Range west of the Basis Meri-.

dian, and the adjoining Sections numbered Thirty, and Thirty-one, in Township numbered Ten in the First Range west of the Basis Meridian of the Land District east of Pearl River, in the Mississippi Territory.

Given under my hand, and seal of office, this fifth day of October, in the year one thousand eight hundred and twelve,

{ SEAL OF THE } { TREASURY. }

(Signed)   ALBERT GALLATIN,
                        Secretary of the Treasury.

A true copy from the original filed in this Office.

EDWARD TIFFIN, Commissioner,

AN ACT

For the relief of Jefferson College, in the State of Mississippi.

SEC. 1. *Be it enacted by the Senate and House of Representatives of the United States of America, in Congress Assembled,* That the Trustees of Jefferson College in the State of Mississippi, be, and they are hereby authorized to relinquish, by a resolution of the Board, all the right, title and interest of said College, in and to certain lands, to be particularly described in said resolution by the sectional numbers, being in Township number ten, of ranges number one and two west, in the District of Lands offered for sale at St. Stephens, heretofore reserved for the use of said College, and an attested copy of said resolution, signed by the President and Secretary of the Board, under the corporate seal of the Institution, shall be placed on file in the General Land Office, and operate as a full release of all claim to said land on the part of said College,

SEC. 2. *And be it further enacted,* That the Board of Trustees of said College, under the superintendence of the Secretary of the Treasury, shall be and is hereby authorized to locate or enter, or cause to be located or entered, in tracts not less in quantity than two sections in one body, such a number of sections, or legal subdivisions of sections, of the unappropriated land of the United States, within the State of Mississippi, as may be equal in number to those which may be relinquished by said Board in virtue of the first section of this act, to be selected, entered or located, either before or after the same may have been offered at public sale, conforming in such entries or locations to the legal subdivisions established by the surveys made, or to be made under the authority of the United States; and such entries or locations shall be made with the Register of the Land Office for the District in which the land so entered or located may lie; and it shall be the duty of such Register to designate such land on the maps and other books in his office in the same manner as lands sold by him, and to issue in each case a certificate of such entry or location, in the form to be prescribed by the Commissioner of the General Land Office, which certificate shall vest a full and complete title, to the land described therein, in Jefferson College, and thereupon a patent shall issue.

Sec. 3. *And be it further enacted,* That the Board of Trustees of Jefferson College be, and they are hereby, authorized and permitted, to sell or lease for any term of years, the land which may be entered or located by virtue of this act, for the benefit of said College, and the deed or deeds of the said Trustees, shall vest a valid title in fee simple in all lands sold by them in virtue of the authority herein conferred: *Provided,* that the proceeds of such sales shall constitute a permanent fund for the use of said College.

Sec. 4. *And be it further enacted,* That to enable the Trustees to secure to the said College all the benefits arising from this act, with as little delay and expense as practicable, they may, and they are hereby authorized, if in their opinion the interests of said Institution would be promoted thereby, to transfer the right of location or entry, conferred by this act, either in whole or in part; and the person or persons legally holding the deed or deeds of transfer, passed under the corporate seal of said College, shall be allowed to make the selection, entry or location, in the manner provided, and in the quantity so transferred, and shall be entitled to receive a certificate, or certificates, from the Register of the proper Land District, and which shall be issued to the legal holder of such deed of assignment as the assignee of Jefferson College, and the title under such certificates shall be accounted and held as valid and complete as if a patent had issued therefor; and all certificates which may be issued by virtue of this act, shall be recorded in the office from which they emanate; and, for each certificate so issued and recorded, the Register shall be entitled to two dollars, to be paid by the party in whose favor such certificate may be issued.

A. STEPHENSON,
Speaker of the House of Representatives.

J. C. CALHOUN,
Vice President of the United States,
and President of the Senate.

Approved April 20, 1832.
ANDREW JACKSON.

CIRCULAR

To the Land Officers of the Several Districts in the State of Mississippi.

GENERAL LAND OFFICE, }
May 14th, 1832. }

Gentlemen,—Herewith is transmitted a copy of an Act of Congress, approved on the 20th April, 1832, entitled *"An Act for the relief of Jefferson College, in the State of Mississippi."*

Under the First Section of this Act, the Board of Trustees of said College are authorized to relinquish to the United States all the right, title, and interest of said College in and to certain lands in the St. Stephens District, heretofore reserved for the use of said College. The Second Section authorizes them to locate or enter, or cause to be located, or entered at any of the Land Offices in the State of Mississippi, a quantity of unappropriated public land, equal to that relinquished by them to the United States, and directs that such entries or locations shall be in tracts not less in quantity than two sections *in one body;* and that they may be made either before or after the same shall have been offered at public sale. The locations may be made in two contiguous sections, four contiguous half sections, eight contiguous quarter sections, or sixteen contiguous half quarter sections. The contiguity must be on the sides or ends of tracts, and not merely points of contact at the corners of tracts. The Register will enter such tracts on his maps and tract book, indicating that the land has been appropriated for the benefit of Jefferson College.

A form of the Certificate to be issued for the entries, under the Second Section of the Act, is herewith transmitted. These certificates are to be transmitted by you to this Office, and thereupon patents will be issued.

Under the provisions of the Fourth Section of the Act, the Trustees of Jefferson College are authorized to transfer their right of location, or entry, either in whole or in part; "and the person or persons legally holding the deed or deeds of transfer, passed under the corporate seal of said College, shall be allowed to make the selection, entry or location in the manner provided, and in the quantity so transferred, and shall be entitled to receive a certificate or certificates from the Register of the proper Land District, and which shall be issued to the legal holder of such deed of assignment, as the assignee of Jefferson College." Such certificate will confer a *complete title.* No patent will therefore be issued under the fourth section of the act. The deeds of transfer, made by the Trustees of the College, must be in favor of some one or more persons for the quantity of two sections, (1280 acres, more or less,) which is required to be located in one body of contiguous tracts, as provided for by the Second Section. Such transfers must be under the corporate seal of the College, and contain the necessary words of a grant conveying a title to real estate in fee. Such deeds of transfer are to be recorded in the office of the Register of the Land Office where the locations or entries are made, and the Register will issue one certificate in favor of the party or parties surrendering any one deed, which certificate, is also to be *recorded in the office of the Register*, as it vests a *complete title*, without a patent from the Government. A form of this certificate is also transmitted. The certificate is to be on parchment. You are requested to provide yourself with a blank book, into which you will record all the deeds of transfer made by the College; and also, all the certificates which you may have to issue under the fourth section of the act.

The deeds of transfer are to be forwarded to, and filed in this office, for safe keeping, and are each to have an endorsement, indicating the date of certificate of title issued thereon under the fourth section of the act—the names of the parties to whom, and the designation of the tract for which such certificate was granted, and the book and pages in which such deed and the certificate are respectively recorded. You will indicate at the foot of your respective monthly abstracts, the locations made under the provisions of this act.

As this office is not aware in what Districts the locations will be made, it has been deemed most proper to transmit the whole number of forms, which will be required in the execution of the act, to the Secretary of the Board of Trustees of Jefferson College, who is requested to distribute them as occasion may require.

I am, very respectfully,
Your obedient servant,
ELIJAH HAYWARD, Commissioner.

To the Register of the Land Office and Receiver of Public Moneys, Mount Salus, Mississippi.

RELINQUISHMENT OF THE LANDS OF JEFFERSON COLLEGE, LOCATED BY THE SECRETARY OF THE TREASURY.

JEFFERSON COLLEGE, April 3, 1833.

Resolved, That, in pursuance of an Act of Congress, passed on the 20th day of April, 1832, entitled *"An Act for the relief of Jefferson College, in the State of Mississippi"*: The BOARD OF TRUSTEES of said College do hereby grant, release, and relinquish forever, unto the United States of America, all the right, title, claim, and interest, of the said College, in and to the following described lands, which were located by the Secretary of the Treasury, on the fifth day of June, in the year one thousand eight hundred and twelve, in pursuance of the Act of Congress, passed on the 20th of February, 1812, entitled *"An Act authorizing the Secretary of the Treasury to locate the lands reserved for the use of Jefferson College, in the Mississippi Territory"*; To wit: Sections One, Two, Three, Four, Five, Six, Seven, Eight,

Nine, Ten, Twelve, Thirteen, Fourteen, Sixteen, Seventeen, Eighteen, Nineteen, Twenty, Twenty-one, Twenty-two, Twenty-three, Twenty-four, Twenty-five, Twenty-six, Twenty-seven, Twenty-eight, Twenty-nine, Thirty, Thirty-one, Thirty-two, Thirty-three, and Thirty-six, and the east half and north-west quarter of Section Eleven, and the north-west and south-west quarters and the west half of the north-east quarter of Section Fifteen, in Township Ten, of Range number Two west; and also Sections Thirty and Thirty-one in Township Ten, Range One west, equal to thirty-five sections and three-eighths of a section, in the District of Lands subject to sale at St. Stephens, Alabama: Saving and reserving the following tracts of land located by the Secretary of the Treasury on the fifth day of June, one thousand eight hundred and twelve, for the use of Jefferson College, which are not intended to be relinquished; viz: the south-west quarter of Section Eleven, and the south-east quarter and east half of the north-east quarter of Section Fifteen, in Township Ten of Range Two west, in the District aforesaid.

RESOLUTION ESTABLISHING THE TERMS, AND AUTHORIZING THE SALES OF THE COLLEGE LANDS.

JEFFERSON COLLEGE, March 11, 1833.

Resolved, That B. L. C. Wailes, agent of Jefferson College, be authorized, until the first of January next, to accept of any proposals which may be made for the purchase of the Lands of Jefferson College, under the provisions of the fourth section of the Act of Congress of the twentieth of April, one thousand eight hundred and thirty-two, for the relief of said College, at the rate of six dollars and a half per acre: one fourth part of the purchase money to be paid in two years from the date of purchase; one fourth in three years; and the balance in one, two, and three years thereafter: the whole to bear interest at the rate of eight per cent. per annum, payable annually; to be secured by joint notes, executed by the principal and securities, made payable at the Planters' Bank of the State of Mississippi, and also by a mortgage upon the land located: the mortgage to be executed at the time of making the location. And the said agent, upon the receipt of notes for the purchase money, so executed, and which shall have been approved by the committee appointed for that purpose, shall be authorized to issue a certificate of sale, in proper form, to the purchaser or purchasers of each tract of two sections, which may be so sold by him.

RESOLUTION AUTHORIZING THE EXECUTION OF DEEDS OF TRANSFER.

Resolved, That B. L. C. Wailes, the agent of Jefferson College, be, and he is hereby authorized, to make and execute, in behalf of the Trustees of said College, such deeds of transfer to the purchasers of the College lands, as may be required under the fourth section of the Act of Congress of the 20th April, 1832, entitled "*An Act for the relief of Jefferson College, in the State of Mississippi.*"

I, A. M. SCOTT, Governor of the State of Mississippi, and President of the Board of Trustees of Jefferson College, do hereby certify, that the resolution, of which the foregoing is a true copy, was adopted by said Board on this day.

Given under my hand and the seal of said College, this eleventh day of March, Anno Domini one thousand eight hundred [SEAL.] and thirty-three.

A. M. SCOTT.

By the President,
Attest, LEVIN WAILES, Secretary.

FORM OF CERTIFICATE OF SALE

Granted to the purchasers of the College lands upon the execution and delivery of their Notes.

No. 4.   JEFFERSON COLLEGE, STATE OF MISSISSIPPI.

IT IS HEREBY CERTIFIED, That in pursuance of the Fourth Section of the Act of Congress, passed on the twentieth day of April, in the year one thousand eight hundred and thirty-two, entitled "*An Act for the relief of Jefferson College, in the State of Mississippi,*" and in conformity with the resolutions of the Board of Trustees, passed on the first day of December, 1832, *Samuel B. Marsh* has purchased from the Board of Trustees of Jefferson College, the right to locate two sections of land, to contain twelve hundred and eighty acres, more or less, at the rate of six dollars and fifty cents per acre; and having executed Notes for the payment of the purchase money, with *James R. Marsh, Thomas Hudnall, and J. C. Griffing*, as securities, payable in the manner following: That is to say,

Six hundred and sixty-five dollars and sixty cents, on the *first* day of *February*, 1834;

Two thousand seven hundred and forty-five dollars and sixty cents, on the *first* day of *February*, 1835;

Two thousand five hundred and seventy-nine dollars and twenty cents, on the *first* day of *February*, 1836;

E

66

One thousand seven hundred and nineteen dollars and forty-six cents, on the *first* day of *February*, 1837;

One thousand six hundred and eight dollars and fifty-four cents, on the *first* day of *February*, 1838;

One thousand four hundred and ninety-seven dollars and sixty cents, on the *first* day of *February*, 1839.

Now, therefore, be it known, That in consideration of the premises, and in conformity with the Act of Congress and the Resolutions of the Board of Trustees of Jefferson College, above recited, I do hereby certify, That the said *Samuel B. Marsh* is entitled to a deed of transfer of the right of the said College to locate two sections, or twelve hundred and eighty acres of land, in the manner prescribed in the Act of Congress above recited, and in conformity with the instructions of the Secretary of the Treasury of the United States, when the Land Offices, contemplated in the late Choctaw cession, shall have been established and organized, and upon the surrender of this Certificate.

Given under my hand and seal, the sixth day of March, A. D. 1833.

B. L. C. WAILES,

[B. L. C. W.]   Agent of Jefferson College.

FORM OF DEED,

Executed by the Agent of the College, on the surrender of the foregoing Certificate of Sale, and delivered at the time of making the location at the Land Office.

THIS DEED OF TRANSFER, made this *twenty-first* day of *October*, in the year of our Lord one thousand eight hundred and thirty-*three*, between the Trustees of Jefferson College, of the Town of Washington, and State of Mississippi, by *B. L. C. Wailes, agent of said College*, of the one part, and *Samuel B. Marsh, of the County of Tallahatchie, and State of Mississippi*, of the other part, witnesseth—That, whereas, by an Act of Congress, passed on the twentieth day of April, in the year one thousand eight hundred and thirty two, entitled "An Act for the relief of Jefferson College, in the State of Mississippi," the Trustees of said College are authorized to transfer the right of locating or entering certain lands granted by the said act, in the manner prescribed therein: And, whereas, the Trustees of said College have, by their resolution of the *eleventh day of March*, 1833, authorized and empowered *B. L. C. Wailes, agent of said College*, to make and execute all such deeds of transfer, as may be required under the fourth section of the act aforesaid : Now, this deed of transfer, witnesseth—That the said Trustees of Jefferson College, by the said *B. L. C. Wailes*, for and in consideration of the premises, and the sum of *ten thousand eight hundred and sixteen dollars,* to the said Trustees of Jefferson College, paid at or before the sealing of these presents, the receipt whereof is hereby acknowledged, have granted, bargained, sold, conveyed, and confirmed, and by the presents DO grant, bargain, sell, convey, and confirm unto the said *Samuel B. Marsh,* his heirs and assigns, *two sections of land, containing twelve hundred and eighty acres,* more or less, to be selected, entered or located by the said *Samuel B. Marsh,* under the provisions of the Act of Congress aforesaid—to have and to hold the said *two sections* of land to the said *Samuel B. Marsh,* his heirs and assigns forever.

In testimony whereof, the said *B. L. C. Wailes, agent* of Jefferson College, has hereunto set his hand, and affixed the corporate seal of said College, on the day and year first above written.

B. L. C. WAILES.   { SEAL OF JEFFERSON COLLEGE. }

Upon the surrender of the foregoing deed to the Register of the Land Office, the purchaser received a certificate or PATENT, executed on parchment in the following form—executing at the same time a mortgage on the land located to the Trustees of Jefferson College.

LAND OFFICE AT CHOCCHUMA, STATE OF MISSISSIPPI. .
No.

IT IS HEREBY CERTIFIED, That in pursuance of the Fourth Section of the Act of Congress, passed on the twentieth day of April, in the year one thousand eight hundred and thirty-two, entitled "An Act for the relief of Jefferson College, in the State of Mississippi," and in conformity with instructions from the Secretary of the Treasury, *Samuel B. Marsh,* of *Tallahatchie* county, assignee of Jefferson College, having deposited, and caused to be recorded in this office, a deed of transfer, passed under the corporate seal of said College, bearing date the *twenty-first* day of *October,* in the year one thousand eight hundred and thirty-*three,* for the quantity of two sections, containing twelve hundred and eighty acres, more or less, the said *Samuel B. Marsh,* assignee of Jefferson College, has this day entered, or located at this office, the following described land, viz : *the south half of section twenty, the east half of the north-east, the north-west quarter, and the west half of the south-west quarter of section twenty-nine, the east half of section thirty, and the north half of section thirty-one,* in Township number *twenty-two,* of Range number *three east,* in the District of Lands subject to sale at *Chocchuma,* containing together *twelve hundred and seventy-six acres and forty-six hundredths of acre.*

NOW, THEREFORE, BE IT KNOWN, That in consideration of the premises, and in conformiy with the Act of Congress above recited, I do hereby certify, That the United States of America have given and granted, and by these presents DO give and grant unto the said *Samuel*

B. Marsh, assignee of Jefferson College, and to *his* heirs, the land above described, to have and to hold the same, together with all the rights, privileges, immunities, and appurtenances, of whatsoever nature thereunto belonging, unto the said *Samuel B. Marsh*, and *his* heirs and assigns forever.

Given under my hand at *Chocchuma*, the *twenty-first* day of *October*, in the year one thousand eight hundred and thirty-*three*.

SAMUEL GWIN,
Register of the Land Office.

ESTATE AND RESOURCES
OF
JEFFERSON COLLEGE,
ON THE FIRST OF AUGUST, 1839.

Real Estate, consisting of about forty-eight acres of land,
  with the College buildings thereon, estimated at $ 59,625 74
Library and Apparatus, - - - - - - - - - - - - - 6,902 25
Bank Stock, viz: in Agricultural Bank, $ 50,000
          Commercial Bank of Natchez, 11,500
                           61,500 00
Cash, - 7,543 53
Debt due from Individuals, for purchase of Natchez lots,   35,025 42
  do. do. for purchase of College lands, &c. - - - - - 74,874 52
Money on loan, - - - - - - - - - - - - - - - - - - 6,200 00
                             $ 251,671 46

The Institution is indebted to the City of Natchez about seventeen thousand dollars; and a few other claims, not exceeding three thousand dollars, are outstanding against it. No estimation is made of the loans of the State about twenty years since; as the Legislature has invariably refused to exact the payment of these loans, they may, perhaps, be considered donations, as they were doubtless originally designed to be.

PHILOSOPHICAL AND CHEMICAL APPARATUS, &c.
OF
JEFFERSON COLLEGE.

Electrical Machine, 18 inch *plate* and appendages.

Do. do. *cylinder.*

Two Air Pumps, brass barrel, with receivers and other appendages, complete.

Telescope, Fraunhoffer's refracting.

Sextant.

Barometer.

Surveyor's Compass.

Pocket Compass.

Case of Mathematical Instruments.

Steam Engine, high pressure.

Electro-Magnetic Rotary, and Railway.

Microscope, *compound.*

Do. *for mineralogical specimens.*

Do. *single.*

Sucking Pump, glass model.

Forcing Pump, do.

Mercury Shower apparatus.

Intermitting Fountain.

Spouting do.

Thermometer, Standard.

Do. Chemical.

Do. Differential.

Do. Pixis, glass scale.

Do. for high steam.

Do. air, and jar.

Do. Lanctorio's.

Do. cylindric bulb.

Electro-Magnetic apparatus, Davenport's rotary.

Do. do. rotary horse shoe.

Do. do. Woolcott's.

Model of the Eye, in brass.

Oersted's apparatus for condensing water.

Hydrostatic Bellows.

Hydrostatic Paradox apparatus.

Barker's Mill, in glass.

Reflective Goniometer.

Common do.

Graphic Mirror.

Camera Obscura.

Kaleidoscope.

Condensing Lens.

Three Prisms.

A variety of Magnets.

Aurora Borealis Tube.

Electric Cannon.

Flask for weighing air.

Mirrors, cylindrical, convex, and concave.

Do. multiplying.

Do. optical deception.

Inclined Planes, with graduated arc and car.

Spirit Level.

Burning Lens.

Witham's Fossil Woods, 24 specimens.

Eight specimens do. for optical purposes.

Models of Primitive Crystals.

Delicate Scales for analysis.

Weights for set of Mechanics.

Geometric Solids.
Model of endless Screw apparatus.
Stand and Rails for illustrating Pendulum.
Centre of Gravity apparatus.
Spur Wheel apparatus, copper.
Levers.
Pulleys.
Wheel and Axle, &c., &c.

———

Galvanic Battery, Cruickshanks' trough, with 80 plates.
Cylindric Batteries, various sizes.
Ampere's Rotary Battery.
De la Rives' Battery and Ring.
Hare's Calorimoter.
Volta's Eudiometer.
Davy's Safety Lamp.
Pyrometer.
Compound Blow Pipe, tube and jet.
Black's Blow Pipe.
Leaden Alembic and Condenser, for fluoric acid.
Globular brass Steam Generator.
Plates for Galvanic Battery.
Large apparatus for decomposing water.
Davy's apparatus for showing transference of acid through alkali.

Apparatus for decomposing salts.
Do. for decomposing acetate of lead.
Apparatus for decomposing water in cylinder, and transferring the same.
Farraday's apparatus for decomposing glauber salt.
Do. do. do. hydriodate of potash.
Wollaston's model of Condensing Engine.
Baume's Hydrometer for alcohol.
Cartier's do. do.
Guy Lussac's do. for salts.
Baume's do. for acids.
Aphlogistic Lamp.
Argand do.
Chilton Magnet, for exhibiting electric spark.
Electro-Galvanic Multiplier.
Self-regulating Reservoir apparatus.
Ampere's Helix.
Exploding Phial for gases.
Apparatus for sulphurous acid.
Pneumatic Cistern.
Hemming's Safety Tube.
Two half-barrel glass Gas-holders, with brass caps, stop cocks, &c.
Eighty rare Chemical Preparations, by Professor Gale, in glass, hermetically sealed.

Together with stoppered and plain Retorts, of glass, porcelain, and iron, of various sizes; Receivers, double tubulated and single, of various sizes; Tripods; Lamp Stands; Furnaces; Lipped and Precipitating Jars; Filtering Cups; Syphons; Syringes; Funnels; Evaporating Dishes; Burners; Stop Cocks; Coupling Screws; Ladles; Receiver Caps; porcelain and iron Mortars; platinum, porcelain, and iron Crucibles; French glass Tubes; dropping Tubes; brass and copper Wire; lead, copper, and tin Tube, &c., &c., &c.; and an extensive supply of Chemical Substances.

MINERALOGICAL AND GEOLOGICAL CABINET.

The specimens are too numerous to be particularized. The Collection includes:

First—A Mineralogical Collection, arranged for studying the science, comprehending a good variety of all the Minerals, with models of the primary forms of all the Crystals, with Goniometers for studying Crystalography, &c., &c.

Second—Geological Cabinet, including a geological alphabet, or collection of specimens, representing all of the principal Formations and Rocks.

Third—Specimens representing the Geology of many parts of the United States.

Fourth—A good variety of Fossils, more especially those of the coal formation, mountain limestone, and red sandstone.

Fifth—A large variety of the Coal Slates of Pennsylvania, containing vegetable impressions, &c.

In the Collection, are found the Metallic Ores, Gold, Silver, Copper, Gallena, Iron, &c., &c., in their various forms; Quartz Crystals, Amethyst, Agates, Jasper, Chalcedony, Garnets, Topaz, Cornelian, Tourmaline, Obsidian, Maibles, Granites, Serpentine, Grenatite, Asbestos, Kyamite, Epidite, Hornblende, Cyanite, Angite, Pyroxene, Tremolite, Brucite, Lepidolite, &c., &c.

Also, forty Maps, Sections, and other Drawings, illustrating on a large scale the animals and vegetables of an ancient world, including views of geological formations, caverns, mines, quarries, &c. &c.

1. De la Beche's Strata.
2. Section of Gneiss in N. York Tunnel.
3. Sectional View of Barren Island.
4. Plesiosaurus Mastodon and Megatherium.
5. Lyall's Map—Changes of Climate.
6. Jupiter Serapis.
7. Pterodactyle.
8. De la Beche's Tabular View of Strata.
9. Vesuvius in 1794.
10. Skeleton of the Mastodon of Peale's Museum.
11. Ichthyosaurus and Plesiosaurus.
12. Geological Map of Italy.
13. Strata, with Basaltic Dykes.
14. Dream Cavern of Derbyshire.
15. Megatherium.

A
HISTORICAL SKETCH
OF
JEFFERSON COLLEGE,

FROM ITS ESTABLISHMENT, IN 1802, TO ITS RE-ORGANIZATION, IN 1839.

Jefferson College was incorporated by an act of the Legislature of the Mississippi Territory, of the 13th May, 1802. It had no endowment, but was to be "supported by voluntary contributions," to which end the Trustees were authorized to receive donations, from citizens and others, and to raise a sum of money by lottery.

On the third of January of the succeeding year, 1803, the Trustees met at the Town of Washington, and organized the Board, by the election of William C. C. Claiborne, Governor of the Mississippi Territory, President; William Dunbar, Vice President, and Felix Hughes, Secretary. On the sixth of June following Alexander Montgomery was elected Treasurer.

"Sensible of the difficulty of the task of erecting an Institution for public education without public funds," the Trustees, at their first meeting, adopted an address to the public, in which they appealed to the patriotism of their fellow citizens, to supply this want by their private liberality, and depicted, in forcible terms, the benefits to be derived from the support of the Institution, and the great advantages of home education.

The Trustees, at the same time, petitioned Congress for aid, "in this first attempt to institute a place of general education for the youth of the Territory, which, by a law of the Legislature, had devolved upon them," an attempt "attended with peculiar impediments, in a community but lately emerged from the lethargic influence of an arbitrary government, averse from principle to the general information of its citizens," a community which would consequently "be tardy in learn-ing the necessity of affording effectual aid to such an object by voluntary contribution."

The appeal to the public was productive of very limited aid, that to Congress was promptly and liberally responded to by a grant, on the third of March, 1803, of a township of land, and some lots of ground in and adjoining the City of Natchez.

A Committee appointed to select a site for the College, having re-commended one on the lands of Mordecai Throckmorton, adjoining Greenville, in Jefferson County, the Board at its meeting, on the fourteenth of March, 1803, concurred in said report; and on the eleventh of April following, convened at Greenville; when the resolu-tion proposing that place for the location of the College, was repealed, and the Board adjourned, to meet at Selsertown, in Adams County, on the sixth of June. At the second meeting, held at Selsertown on the twenty-fifth of July, 1803, the Committee "for viewing the different sites offered as donations to Jefferson College," reported a resolution, recommending one in the vicinity of that place, as most eligible. The Board, however, refused to concur in the recommendation, but accepted a donation of lands, offered by John and James Foster, and Randall Gibson, adjoining the Town of Washington, and embracing Ellicott's Spring, so called from a former encampment of the party of Andrew Ellicott, commissioner of the United States, for receiving possession of the Mississippi Territory from the Spanish Authorities, and for determin-ing the line of demarkation between the United States, and the Province of West Florida.

The Trustees then addressed a petition to the Legislature, praying that said grounds should be fixed by law as the permanent site for Jef ferson College, which was accordingly done by the act of the eleventh of November, 1803. These donations were subsequently extended, and the Committee appointed for the purpose of procuring the title deeds therefor, and for superintending the survey of said grounds, re-ported, on the thirty-first of March, 1804, a plan thereof, embracing about forty-seven acres.

A scheme for the lottery contemplated by the Charter, was prepared and reported by Mr. Dunbar, the Vice President, in June, 1803, and an effort was made and persevered in for two years, to raise a fund by this means, to put the Institution into operation; but the attempt proving ineffectual, was abandoned, and the money obtained for the tickets sold, was directed to be refunded.

The Trustees having met in pursuance of adjournment at the Hospital, in the City of Natchez, on the twenty-eighth of January,

1804, Col. Cato West, Secretary, exercising the powers, and performing the duties of Governor of the Mississippi Territory, then reported "that the lots in the City of Natchez, and an out lot adjoining the same, granted to the College by Congress, had been duly located, and that upon these lots were several valuable buildings." Steps were immediately taken to render these buildings available, by means of leases, towards supplying a revenue for the College. The Trustees, however, were thwarted in this attempt, being met by the claim of an individual, and of the authorities of the City of Natchez, to the same property.— The active interference of these adverse claimants, procured the passage of an Act of Congress for *suspending* the location, and at a succeeding session it was re-granted to the City, saving, however, the right of the College. Overtures were made ineffectually by the Trustees, for the repair of the buildings in question, and the erection of others on the grounds, so as to render them productive, whilst the controversy as to the eventual title was pending. The buildings consequently went to decay, and were destroyed.

Appeals were made to the public for aid in vain, and finally, on the twenty-first of December, 1805, a loan from the Legislature was prayed for, with like result. From this period, the Trustees were not re-assembled until the twelfth of April, 1810, a period of more than four years.

Towards the close of this interval, the "*Washington Academy*" had been established and was conducted by the Rev. James Smylie.— Temporary frame buildings had been erected, or were in the progress of construction, on the lands of the College, by means of subscriptions, raised for that purpose. A conference between the Boards of the two Institutions, resulted in a transfer of these buildings, and subscriptions to Jefferson College, the latter institution assuming all the contracts and engagements of the former. Among these engagements, was the drawing of a lottery set on foot by the Washington Academy.

Much difficulty was experienced in disposing of the tickets, to an amount to justify the drawing, even when offered on a credit. This occasioned several postponements of the time appointed for that purpose, and it did not take place until November, 1811. Fortunately for the Institution, the larger prizes were drawn to the unsold tickets, otherwise it would have been deeply embarrassed by the transaction. As it was, if it did not result in actual loss, no gain ensued to the College, and the Trustees found themselves under the necessity, in the following year, of directing suits against the purchasers of tickets, who had failed to pay for them.

Having prepared the buildings on the College grounds for the purpose, the Trustees gave public notice of the opening of "an Academy, under the superintendence of Doct. Edwin Reese, assisted by Mr. Samuel Graham, on the first of January, 1811."

Thus nearly nine years after the date of the charter, the Trustees, on failure of the means of putting the Institution into operation on a larger scale, *commenced* it on the footing of an humble Academy.— Upon this unpretending organization it continued for many years, under the charge of various instructors, generally respectable in character and attainments, and, in many instances, well fitted for the duties of their respective stations, meeting the demands of the neighboring community as a preparatory School, and depending almost wholly upon the avails of the tuition charges.

In the mean time, the Trustees resumed their efforts to render the endowments of the Institution available. An investigation of the title of the College to the lots, located in the City of Natchez, was instituted, and all attempts at an amicable adjustment of their conflicting claims, between the Corporations of the City and College failing, a suit at law was directed for the recovery of that property, the Trustees, deeming it "a dereliction of duty longer to delay a judicial investigation of a question involving so materially the welfare of the College." This suit was commenced about the close of the year 1813.

In 1812, Commissioners were appointed throughout the Territory for the purpose of recovering such escheated property as the College might be found entitled to, the Legislature having granted it all escheats for the period of ten years.

The authority of the Legislature to declare such forfeitures without the sanction of Congress, was questioned, and an unsuccessful application was made to the National Legislature, to confirm the enactment of the Territorial Assembly in relation to escheats. Nevertheless the right of the College was successfully asserted in two instances, and about five or six thousand dollars was realized in those cases. In two other cases, each involving a large property, the College was unsuccessful, and subjected to heavy expenses by the prosecution of its claims.

Under the authority of the act of Congress, passed the twentieth of February, 1812, the Secretary of the Treasury of the United States, upon the application of the Trustees, located on the fifth of June, 1812, the township of land granted to the College in 1803. The land selected was situated on both sides of the Tombigby River, about twenty miles above St. Stephens. An agent was appointed to lease out a portion of this land, and to collect rents from intruders who had settled upon it. The low rates and liberal credit upon which the Government lands were obtainable at this period, and the impunity with which they were extensively occupied by intruders, afforded little prospect of realizing much profit for the College, from its right of *leasing* this land.

At the session of the Legislature of the Territory, in December, 1816, the sum of six thousand dollars was appropriated to be paid to the Trustees in four annual instalments, for the purpose of employing a suitable person to place at the head of the College. A belief was entertained, that by engaging and retaining, for a period corresponding with the term of this appropriation, an individual of established reputation and known ability, a character would be earned for the Institution, that would in future command a patronage sufficiently great to maintain its respectability and usefulness.

Mr. James M'Allister, a Scotch gentleman, then filling a professorship at Bardstown, Kentucky, and for many years advantageously known in the United States for his profound learning, was accordingly engaged, and attracted to the Institution a considerable accession of students.

Mr. M'Allister took charge of the Institution in June, 1817, and in August following the Trustees contracted for the building of the East wing of the College edifice, preparatory to the anticipated extension of its operations.

About the close of the year 1818, the attention of the Trustees was again directed to the Alabama lands. Emigration to that State had become very great, the staple of the South commanded a high price, and a spirit of speculation soon created a demand for cotton lands, which enhanced their prices to a rate before unexampled. At this favorable juncture, the Trustees despatched an Agent to St. Stephens, for the purpose of leasing every alternate section of these lands. Leases were effected at favorable rates, for the term of ninety nine years, and about eight thousand dollars was realized as the first instalment, and the remaining instalments of those leases, amounting to more than twenty five thousand dollars, payable in two, four, and six years, were calculated upon with the utmost confidence, at the periods at which they were payable. In this improved aspect of the affairs of the College, the Trustees deemed it incumbent upon them to anticipate, for the benefit of the Institution, some of its resources, and upon the faith of which a loan, eventually amounting to nine thousand dollars, was obtained from Bank, and together with a further sum of four thousand dollars loaned by the State, was applied towards hastening the completion of the buildings which were in the progress of erection.

The expectations of the Trustees of further revenue from the Tombigby lands, however sanguine, were, in a few years, proven to be utterly fallacious.

The Government of the United States found it expedient, in 1820, to adopt measures for the reduction of the enormous debt due from the purchasers of the public domain. The price of the public lands was reduced, and the credit system abolished. To facilitate the extinguishment of the land debt, liberal discounts were offered from time to time, and the privilege of relinquishing the lands purchased was accorded.

These measures were rendered necessary by the pecuniary embarrassment and distress attending one of those revulsions, which infallibly succeed the wild operations of a speculating community, unseasonably and unduly stimulated by visionary expectations of acquiring sudden wealth. The great depreciation in the value of lands which ensued, disposed those who had it in their power, gladly to surrender to the Government their injudicious purchases. It was in vain that the Trustees surpassed the munificient liberality of Congress, and offered an abatement of *one half* of the amount due from *their* debtors. All, with one inconsiderable exception, preferred forfeiting their leases, a measure to which they were the more inclined, as the greater portion of the land was found to be utterly worthless. Thus was the chief source of income of the College destroyed, with all hope of future revenue from that unhappy location. The Institution was consequently burthened with a heavy debt, which it had no means of discharging, and which the Trustees, and a few liberal friends of the Institution, were soon under the necessity of assuming individually.

For years it was harrassed by its creditors, and executions even levied upon the College edifice, and the "Commons" in the City of Natchez.

Not only in its finances, during this period were the Trustees doomed to disappointment. A religious convention of the clergy of all denominations, assembled about the close of the year, 1818, at Washington. The Institution being under the patronage of no exclusive sect, the religious opinions of Mr. M'Allister, then at its head, however unobtrusive or unknown, were chosen for animadversion, and the Institution was publicly and bitterly denounced by the Convention, and an injury done it which the able and indignant response of the Trustees was insufficient entirely to repair.

Nor did the appointment of a clergyman (the Rev. R. F. N. Smith,) who was subsequently associated with Mr. M'Allister, find more favor with the public, than his co-adjutor with the Convention. When the means, appropriated for maintaining them in their stations, was exhausted, the patronage of the community affording no adequate means of support, their connection with the College was dissolved, Mr. Smith retiring first, by the resignation of his Professorship. From the retirement of Mr. M'Allister, in June, 1821, an Acadamy was generally kept up, under the charge of various Instructors, on the same scale and footing as before his appointment.

Destitute of resources and burthened with debt, it was idle to expect that the Institution could be advantageously conducted. Yet much dissatisfaction was manifested by the public, without any show of a willingness on its part to provide for the discharge of its embarrassments, or for its future support. It was assailed in the Legislature, at the session held in January, 1825, and a suit against it, menaced for the recovery of the money loaned it many years before: a measure, however, which the majority of the Legislature refused to countenance.

" To afford an opportunity to the Legislature of placing the Institution more immediately under its control and management, and to give to it that patronage and support which would be due to it as a State Institution," the Trustees proposed at the next session of the Legislature, in January, 1826, a modification of their charter. The act of the thirtieth of January, 1826, was accordingly passed, and accepted by the Trustees. The right of filling vacancies in the Board, conferred by that act, has since been exercised by the Legislature.

In May, 1826, the Trustees were notified by their Attorney, that the Selectmen of the City of Natchez had taken, or intended to take, an appeal to the Supreme Court of the United States, in the suit, commenced in 1813, for the property in the City, claimed by the College, and in which judgments had been rendered in favor of the College, in the several Courts of the State, to which it had been carried. The difficulty of prosecuting this suit, even at home, in the straitened circumstances of the Institution, where the fees of its Attorneys were necessarily made dependent upon the recovery of the property in question, was sufficiently formidable. But the necessity, after a legal contest of ten years, of pursuing the case to the Supreme Court of the United States, at Washington City, without the means of retaining counsel thus remote, was vexatious and embarrassing in the extreme.— A compromise with the City was proposed, and a Committee of conference appointed. The death of the Professor in charge of the College occurred at this moment, and a Committee appointed to engage the services of a successor, reported that no person of suitable qualifications could be found to accept the situation, on any inducements which the Board had it in its power to offer. The doors of the Institution were necessarily closed for a time, to the discontent of the public, and the hazard incurred of further alienating the good feelings of the Legislature. Under circumstances so imperious, the Trustees had no alternative but to terminate the controversy with the City of Natchez, at any sacrifice.

The Committee in behalf of the College, was accordingly authorized to submit distinct propositions of compromise to the City, and, after a protracted negotiation of nearly a year, between the two Boards, definitive terms were agreed upon, and formally accepted by the Selectmen of the City, on the 15th May, 1827.   Subsequent misunderstanding, however, in the execution of the deed, protracted the negotiation two months longer.

The magnitude of this claim, its great importance in a pecuniary view to the College, at the time it was granted, and the pernicious and depressing influence which the controversy for its recovery, had upon the fortunes of the College, demands, before the subject is dismissed, some notice of the claims or titles so unfortunately brought into confliction.

The title of Jefferson College is based upon locations, made by the Governor and acting Governor of the Mississippi Territory, in December, 1803, under the act of Congress, of the 3d of March preceding, authorizing such location, and making the reservation for the use of the College.   Being part of the public domain ceded by the Spanish Government to the United States, the right of Congress to make the grant, was unquestionable.   That it was a part of the domain so ceded, is proven by the evidence of Mr. Girault, formerly an officer of the Spanish Government, who deposed, before the Board of Commissioners, that the Priest's House, on the lots located within the City, now the Court House square, which had been previously occupied by the Catholic Clergy, was delivered, at the change of Government, to the officers of the United States, as public property, and subsequently used by the Legislature, and the Courts of the Mississippi Territory.

The out lot, located in front of the City, it appears, was reserved for the purposes of the Government, and occupied in part by public buildings.   The Spanish Hospital was here situated, and upon it also, a house for the residence of the Governor, was partially erected.   It also became clearly the property of the United States, at the change of government, and was therefore subject to the disposition of Congress.

Mr. Dunbar's claim extended to the out lot only.   It was founded on a Spanish patent executed on the 19th April, 1797, *subsequent to the treaty of cession,* and was filed with the Board of Commissioners for adjudicating land titles, and rejected.

A confirmation was unsuccessfully sought from Congress, on the ground that the grant to him, although made after the title of Spain was alienated, should be recognized, being dissimilar to other grants, as it was made in compensation for services rendered as an officer of the Spanish Government, and inasmuch as the lot in question was the *private property* of the Spanish Crown.   By the purchase of the materials, or remains of a market house situated on a part of this property, Mr. Dunbar put himself in possession under his claim, and continued such occupancy for several years.

Without the color of title, the City of Natchez attempted to wrest this grant from the College, by intercepting it, as it were, between the passage of the act of Congress, and the consummation of the title by location, and, with this view, it succeeded in procuring the passage of an act of Congress for suspending the location, too late, however, to accomplish the object, the location being made in due form, in December, 1803, whilst the act for suspending it was not passed until the March following.

The City authorities now set up a claim before the Board of Commissioners, and the presumed intention of Governor Gayose, in laying off the town, to reserve this property for a military parade ground, and a public walk for the inhabitants, was urged in support of their pretensions. The value to be attached to the intentions, or even verbal declarations of the commandant, as sustaining the claim of the City, will be inferred from the fact, that the "Spanish Government of Louisiana never did grant lands by parole, and that a few years occupancy of lands did not, under that, or any other civilized government, impart a right of common, or create a title by prescription." · The corporation of Natchez had not been two years in existence, and, during that period, the occupancy of part of the property claimed is proven to have been in behalf of Mr. Dunbar. Having been permitted to use occasionally a building on the lot within the City, *after* the change of Government for City purposes, seems to have been the basis of its claim to that part of the property in controversy.

The claim of the corporation of Natchez, was rejected by the Commissioners, and we find the City then a suppliant before Congress, "pretending to no legal title, but asking the grant as a boon from the United States."

Congress, it will be seen, from the report of the Committee to whom the matter was referred, was duly sensible of the importance and value of these lots to the City, and exhibited the strongest disposition to comply with its wishes, "the only obstacle to which," in the language of the Committee, was "the previous grant to the College."

By the act of the 21st April, 1806, (three years after the grant to the College,) Congress yielded so far to the importunities of the City, as to "vest in the corporation of the City of Natchez, the ground between Front Street and the Mississippi River, *so as not to affect the legal or equitable claim of any individual, or body corporate,*" and on the 31st March, 1808, two lots within the City were vested, in like manner, and *with the same reservations.*

When, on the 12th September, 1813, the Attorney of the College made a demand of possession of the Selectmen, the claim of the City was asserted as existing then, "under the several acts of Congress," and the Trustees were called upon to waive their suit, in order to avoid "disagreeable personal sensations between the members of the two Boards."

Upon pretensions so flimsy as these, the City withheld possession from the College, and, by the aid of the law's delay, protracted a suit through a period of ten years, and finally, after a year spent in negotiation, profiting by the necessities of the College, forced the Trustees into a most disadvantageous compromise, by which a portion of the property in dispute was yielded to the College *twenty-four* years after it was granted by Congress.

By the terms of this compromise, an additional street was laid out, and the original streets of the City extended through the commons, a promenade of one hundred and twenty feet in width, along the entire front of the City, was reserved from sale, and the residue was to be sold by the Trustees, and thirty per cent. of the nett proceeds paid to the City, which, on its part, was to construct an aqueduct along the whole extent of the property, and otherwise to improve it. The claim to the lots *within* the City, had been compromised as early as the year 1817, the College receiving five thousand dollars therefor, that property being desired for the purpose of erecting upon it the present Court House of the County, the seat of justice having been removed about that time from Washington.

The lots were speedily laid off, and put into market, and a few sales were effected, but at rates so extremely low, as to determine the Committee charged with the matter to suspend the sales, until further instructed by the Board. The whole of this property was not disposed of, until the year 1836, and then on a credit of three years, the last instalment falling due the first of January, 1839. Property having risen considerably, the last sales were made at greatly improved prices, yet far short of the value it speedily attained.

Less than half of the proceeds of those sales has yet been realized, and as nearly nine years transpired before the sale of this property was wholly effected, but little relief was afforded thereby to the exigencies of the Institution. The Trustees were consequently under the necessity of obtaining loans, at different times, on the personal responsibility of a few of the members, to discharge an execution levied upon the College edifice and to enable them to make some repairs, and erect a building for the accommodation of a Steward, preparatory to the reopening of the Institution, arrangements being made to organize it somewhat on the plan of the National Academy at West Point.

In the mean time, the Legislature had under consideration the subject of a general system of education for the State, and authorized the Executive, at its session in February 1829, " to appoint three Agents to enquire into all the means and resources in the State, applicable to the purposes of general education; to confer with the Trustees of Jefferson College, and ascertain the condition and prospects of the Institution; and whether it was practicable, and on *what terms*, the Trustees would surrender the charter to the State."

The conference accordingly took place on the 27th October, 1829, and an address, setting forth their views at large, was presented by the Agents, accompanied by several interrogatories propounded by them; as to the dimensions and arrangements of the College building; the endowments and available funds; the number and character of the Professors; its future prospects; the expediency of surrendering the Charter; and if the surrender was deemed inexpedient, what report the Agents should make to the Legislature, as to the money loaned to the Institution.

Although in some of the topics discussed in their address, and the last interrogatory, the Agents clearly transcended the authority with which they were clothed, yet the whole subject in its widest range, was met by a full and frank disclosure of the condition and prospects of the Institution. Pains were taken to assemble a full Board, to deliberate upon the communication of the Agents, and especially those members who, rarely attending the meetings of the Trustees, were supposed to be indifferent at least to the interests of the Institution, if not inclined to second the views of the Agents in the surrender of the Charter. Indeed the oldest and most zealous of the members, those who had devoted years to its service, and had sustained it through its most trying embarrassments, wearied with the thankless task which had visited upon them a full share of vexation and opprobium, evinced a determination of opposing no obstacle to the measure. The temper of the Board assembled on this occasion, was most favorable to the desires of the Agents. The investigation, however, given the subject by the Committee appointed to prepare a reply on behalf of the Trustees, satisfied not only the Trustees, but the Agents themselves, of the utter inexpediency, if not impracticability, of the measure. It would perhaps, be unnecessary, if the space allotted to this sketch would admit of it, to refer to all the topics embraced in that reply, the less so, as it formed part of the report of the Agents to the Legislature, which was printed, and is preserved in the archives of the State.

As to the proposed surrender of the Charter, it was shown, "that the proposition involved not merely the annihilation of Jefferson College, but the forfeiture of its resources, and consequently could confer no benefit to any other Institution, though established in its name.— That it could not, by the clearest principle of law, transmit its revenues or endowments to an Institution erected in its stead; for, as to

all purposes to which they were designed, they would necessarily fail
with the demise of the Corporation in which they were originally
vested."

. The tenure by which the property of the Institution was held, for-
bid it. The grant of the township of land, and the Natchez property,
was to a specific institution, "*Jefferson College,*" established, "*in its
permanent site,*" by the Legislature, at Washington, the site itself conveyed to it for the purpose of erecting a College thereon, and for the
use of the same as a public School, and for no other purpose whatever.
If the existence of Jefferson College was terminated by the surrender
of its franchises, its site, with the buildings erected thereon, would re-
vert to the original donors. The land in the Tombigby, if it did not re-
vert to the original grantor, would escheat to the State of Alabama, and
the Natchez property, from the nature of the compromise under which
it was held, would be lost, and would go inevitably to the City of Natchez, Congress, after the grant to the College, having regranted it to
the City.

It was asked, "how far such an act of suicide on the part of the
Corporation, would benefit the State, and in what degree it would aid
the general system of education proposed to be established."

The Agents were reminded, that the Trustees had already voluntarily
placed the Institution under the immediate control of the Legislature,—
yielded to it the right of appointing the Trustees, and placed at the head of
the Board the Executive of the State,—thereby entitling it to the patronage and consideration due to a State Institution. In conclusion, it was
intimated that the Trustees would readily yield the *management* of the
Institution to the hands of those who might be so fortunate as to enjoy,
in a higher degree, the confidence of the Legislature. When the
Legislature assembled again, the Institution was reorganized, and in
operation on a plan which proved highly attractive and popular.

The prospect of realizing much revenue from the Natchez property
being remote, the Trustees had found it necessary to resort to some other
means of conducting the Institution. It was believed that a system of
education like that pursued at West Point, might be advantageously
engrafted upon the Collegiate course; that its practical and scientific
character, conjoined with the fascinating, wholesome, and manly exercise, afforded by the military feature of that system, would find favor
with the public and be productive of much benefit. *The experiment*
was determined upon, the more readily as it was ascertained that it
could be put in practice on a highly respectable scale, under the government of individuals eminently fitted for the task, and without any further pecuniary charge upon the Institution, than that required by the
preparation and repair of the College buildings, to adapt them to more

enlarged operations. An agreement was accordingly entered into, for the term of five years, with Mr. E. B. Williston and Major John Holbrook, the first as President, and the latter in capacity of Superintendent of the scientific and military department. These gentlemen were practically familiar with the system, having filled professorships in the different Academies established by Capt. Alden Patridge, formerly Superintendent at West Point, and by whom they were recommended to the Trustees.

They engaged to employ, at their own charge, a number of competent professors and instructors, adequate to the operations of the College; to provide good commons, under the direction of an attentive and efficient Steward; and to be dependent wholly for remuneration for their services upon the success of their own exertions. It is due to the memory of those gentlemen, to say, that they discharged their duties with much energy and ability; that they retained in their service a full faculty, composed of individuals, as exemplary in their moral character, as they were talented and devoted in the performance of their duties; and that their engagements generally were fulfilled with a fidelity most creditable and praise-worthy.

The success of this experiment was eminent, and, for the first time since its establishment, the Institution was viewed with pride and gratification. A large number of students repaired to it;—their attainments were varied and useful, and their progress and deportment afforded much pleasure to their friends.

The College, under this arrangement, was opened on the first Monday of December, 1829. In April, 1832, the President, Mr. Williston, from his rapidly declining health, found it necessary, greatly to the regret of the Trustees, to resign his station in the Institution. And in August following, Major Holbrook, who succeeded him in the Presidency, died. In these gentlemen, the Institution sustained a loss at that time irreparable.

In the latter part of the year 1830, the Trustees forwarded a memorial to Congress, praying for permission to change the location of the lands of the College on the Tombigby, with the view of selecting others, within the State, in the district of country recently acquired by cession from the Indians. Nothing in behalf of the Institution was accomplished, if attempted, at the succeeding session of Congress. The Trustees, however, determined to renew their application, and to appoint an Agent to attend to the details of the business, and to promote the interests of the Institution, by his presence at Washington City.

Provided with the memorial of the Trustees, and having prepared a bill to embrace the objects sought, the Agent arrived at the seat of government on the 17th day of March, 1832, and on the 20th day of the following month, was in possession of the act of Congress for the relief of the College, approved by the President. The success of this mission far exceeded the expectations of the most sanguine. The unusual and important privileges conferred by this act, greatly enhanced its value, and facilitated its execution. By it the Trustees were authorized to relinquish the Tombigby land, *in whole or in part;* to locate other lands in the State of Mississippi, either *before or after* they should have been offered at public sale; to make the location, not as heretofore, in one entire township, but in tracts of two sections; those tracts, too, not confined to sectional lines, but to be selected, if desired in contiguous legal subdivisions of sections, so as to admit of the most convenient form, and be readily adapted to the natural advantages of almost any position. The Trustees were also authorized *to sell* the land located, in whole or in part, or to *transfer the right of location.* To avoid delay, prevent controversy, and to secure effectually the rights of the College, the Register's certificate of location was made equivalent to a patent executed by the President, and conferred a full and complete title to the land located. Several features of this act are essentially novel in their character: they were incorporated in it from a long acquaintance with the operation of the land system of the United States, and were intended to obviate some obstacles, that it was foreseen, would arise in its execution.

By some of these provisions, it was sustained against the combinations of speculators, associated in land companies, who might otherwise have succeeded at least in postponing its execution, until there was little land left worthy of appropriation. A higher value and consequently a preference was given to the College claims in the market, by means of the latitude allowed in the mode of locating them over other descriptions of claims arising under the Indian treaty, and the assurance of an undisturbed title was found in that unexampled and important provision, which *perfected the title* at the moment of location, by means of the Register's *patent certificate.*

The township of land on the Tombigby was visited and explored by the Agent, for the purpose of ascertaining to what portion of it the title of the College had been alienated under the leases of 1818, and if any part of it was of sufficient value to be retained. Only five eighths of a section of that land was found to have been finally disposed of, and the Trustees eventually determined to relinquish the whole of the remainder of the township.

The Agent was authorized to advertise for proposals for the purchase of the right of location under the fourth section of the act for the relief of the College, and subsequently to sell and convey that right, at the rate of six dollars and fifty cents per acre, payable in instalments in six years, with interest at the rate of eight per cent. per annum from the date of sale. The whole quantity was sold between the first of March and the sixth of August, 1833, but all the locations made at the Land Offices at Chocchuma, Columbus, and Mount Salus, at different periods, under the superintendence of the Agent, were not effected until August, 1834.

Mortgages upon the land were executed to the College, at the time of making the locations, joint notes, with satisfactory personal security, having been previously given. The last note due for this land, was payable on the sixth of August last. In one instance only, have the payments been wholly completed, but, in every instance, with two exceptions only, a portion of the debt has been paid, although the payments have been retarded by the unparralleled embarrassments of the country during the two past years. The whole debt is regarded as *perfectly* secure. With a view of providing a regular income, to meet some of the current expenses of the Institution, at an early period, some of these notes, to the amount of about fifty thousand dollars, were discounted, and converted into Bank stock.

The passage of the law for the relief of the College, became speedily known to the public; and representations as to its highly favorable provisions, produced very exaggerated notions, not merely as to the value of the grant, but vague opinions were generally afloat, among those who could not comprehend, or would not examine the subject, that immense sums were poured at once into the coffers of the College, and that the Trustees had nothing more to do than rear up at once a splendid Institution.

Nor were the Trustees themselves, in the first flush of success, to many of them unexpected, quite prepared to temper the ardor which impelled them to the fulfilment of the public expectations, by a dispassionate survey of the measures yet to be adopted, or to contemplate with patience any delay in the full accomplishment of their wishes.— A conscious independence immediately manifested itself in a proposition "*to change the system of education,*" and to obtain a relinquishment of the lease of Major Holbrook, a measure which contemplated of course an immediate, and, in fact, a premature assumption of all the charges of conducting the Institution.

It was not long to be disguised, however, that the lands to be located were *yet to be surveyed;* that the Land Offices were not yet established; and when, to the period necessary to effect this, the term of credit, which would perhaps be required upon the sales, was added, an interval would be found quite sufficient for cool deliberation and dispassionate action.

It was therefore determined, to permit the existing order of things to remain undisturbed. The lamented death of Major Holbrook, however, which soon occurred, terminated the contract with the College, and made it necessary to provide a successor.

It being ascertained that Capt. Patridge was willing to accept the Presidency of the College, he was accordingly appointed, Professor Ransom, one of Major Holbrook's assistants, having provisional charge of the Institution until his arrival.

The terms of agreement were similar to those entered into with Messrs. Williston and Holbrook, the Board, however, retaining a control in the appointment of Professors, and limiting the rates of tuition and boarding. This arrangement was speedily dissolved, the views of Capt. Patridge as to salary and emoluments, and the compensation of assistants, not being in consonance with those of the Board, or consistent with the available means of the Institution. His wishes, however, as to the control to be exercised by him, *and his residence to the North during a great portion of the year,* were most objectionable, and precluded any further engagement with him. He remained only a few months in charge of the College.

The Trustees then determined to employ three Professors at fixed salaries. Two of the gentlemen appointed, arrived and entered upon their duties on the 11th November, 1833. The number employed was subsequently increased to four. This arrangement continued for some years, with occasional changes in the Professorships, as they became necessary, and with such increase of salary as the available means of the Institution would allow. One of these gentlemen, Mr. Charles L. Dubuisson, was advanced to the Presidency on the 6th June, 1835, and his salary fixed at two thousand dollars, which was subsequently increased to three.

On the 2nd of June, 1835, the first appropriation was made for the foundation of a library. The Institution had never before been in a condition to devote any of its resources to this object. The small commencement previously made, arose from donations, chiefly from Congress.

A series of daring incendiary attempts were made shortly after the commencement of the second term in 1836, to destroy the College buildings by fire. On several occasions fire was communicated to the principal College edifice, in various apartments, from the basement to the attic, which was fortunately discovered in time to arrest the flames, although on two occasions it narrowly escaped destruction. The incendiary, evidently aware of the awakened vigilance of the Faculty and Students, then transferred, with more success, the scene of his operations to an out-building, which, being fired, communicated with an extensive kitchen connected with the Steward's Department, and both were destroyed. By great exertions of the citizens of the town, who promptly repaired to the spot, the Steward's house, a large frame building of a very combustible nature, and the College edifice were saved, although frequently in flames. The contiguity of the Steward's House to the College, and the apprehension that these attempts would be persevered in, or renewed, with the certainty that the former, if burned, would involve the whole in common destruction, induced the Board to direct it to be taken down and removed. Although a large reward for the discovery and apprehension of the incendiary was offered, and several servants were arrested, and underwent an examination, nothing was developed which tended to remove the mystery, in which this affair continues to be shrouded.

The Institution had for some time been declining, and its prosperity or utility, by no means accorded with the number or ability of the Faculty employed, or with the pecuniary means devoted to its support; a circumstance which pressed itself so forcibly and painfully upon the notice of the Trustees, as to demand an enquiry into the causes to which it was to be attributed. A Committee was accordingly appointed to make the investigation. In the report made by the Committee in October, 1837, the depressed state of the Institution was attributed, in part, to a relaxation of discipline, a want of cordial co-operation on the part of the Faculty, as well as the interruption of the duties of the President, by absence and domestic afflictions : but chiefly to the prevalent feeling of partiality, and veneration for the time-honored and distinguished institutions of the North, which impelled most parents to resort to them for the education of their sons, attaching a high value to the honors derived from those venerated shrines, from which have issued so many distinguished men, whose names have shed a lustre upon the history of their country. The abandonment of the West Point system, with the facilities it afforded for the acquisition of scientific and practical knowledge, which had recommended it to the *mass* of the community, was not without its influence. Those who desired a home education, saw no peculiar inducements to resort to an Institution no longer distinguished from the ordinary classical schools of this, and the adjacent States.

At the suggestion of the Committee, the Board determined that, should there not be a manifest improvement in the condition of the Institution, or a decided increase of patronage, previous to the next session, it would be high time to return to that system which experience had proven to be the most popular and efficient yet adopted. The investigation of a subsequent Committee, occupying in part the same grounds, exhibited a lamentable decline in its operations, and the reduction of the number of Students to *twenty-three!* only five of that number being in the College proper, less than two to each Professor, "who, for want of employment, had been compelled to volunteer as *assistants* to the Instructor in the preparatory department."

At the close of the session, in March, 1838, the President determining to resume the profession of the law, in which he had previously engaged, retired from the station he occupied, accompanied by the good wishes of the Trustees.

The resignation of all the members of the Faculty, at the same time, afforded the Board a much desired opportunity of reorganizing the Institution. The better to prepare for this, it was determined to await a fuller developement of its resources, and to apply the unappropriated and accumulating income, in the interval, to the erection of commodious and extensive buildings. With this view the operations of the College proper, were suspended for one year, during which period, however, the Preparatory School was carried on, under the charge of an efficient and competent rector. In the erection and repairs of buildings, and in enclosing and improving the College grounds, to fit them for future operations, the Board expended about twenty-five thousand dollars.

A reference to the rules and regulations for the government of the Institution, which precede this sketch, now printed, as amended, with a view to the re-organization, will fully explain the nature and scope of a system adopted with great unanimity at an unusually large meeting of the Board, at which the Governor of the State presided. It will be seen that ample provision is made for maintaining the regular College course on the most extended scale, whilst the scientific feature of the Institution is more fully developed, or, in other words, is more comprehensive and thorough, than is usual in most Colleges. The accomplishments of topography and drawing, becoming daily more essential, if not necessary branches of education, are added, and the military discipline introduced furnishes a system of police, a mode of exercise, and a means of recreation productive of the most beneficial results.